Bristol Radical Pa

CW00787790

Steps Against War

Resistance to World War 1 in Bedminster

Emma Byron and Trevor Houghton

ISBN 978-1-911522-55-3

Bristol Radical History Group. 2020.
www.brh.org.uk
brh@brh.org.uk

Contents

Acknowledgements

We would like to thank the following people who aided us with the research for this pamphlet: Roger Ball, Lois Bibbings, Jeremy Clarke, Mary Dobbing, June Hannam, Nicholas Hiley, Cyril Pearce and Mike Richardson. And all the history walk project participants who contributed to the research.

Thanks also to Barbara Segal, Richard Musgrove, Mike Levine, Richard Grove and Mike Richardson for their work preparing it for publication.

Introduction

> I will not obey any military order; I would rather die. I am guilty according to the law but not guilty according to justice.

These are the words of George Abraham Smith, a carpenter of 68 Greville Road, Bedminster as reported in the *Western Daily Press* on 8th June 1916. He had been arrested under the Military Service Act 1916 for failing to report for duty as a soldier. He was a conscientious objector resisting conscription. George was one of at least 40 Bedminster men who refused to fight in the First World War.

This pamphlet takes its title from *Steps Against War*, a history walk with puppets and songs that was performed in Bedminster, Bristol in April 2019. This was a community production led by Otherstory, a puppetry company, in collaboration with the Remembering the Real World War 1 group and supported by the National Lottery through the Heritage Fund. The walk used the medium of puppetry to tell the untold stories of Bedminster people who resisted the First World War, and who refused to kill.

Steps Against War developed out of research by members of Remembering the Real World War 1, and research workshops where local people investigated what happened in Bedminster. The work of Cyril Pearce in researching and compiling *the Pearce Register,* a listing of all the known conscientious objectors in the UK, underpins much of what we have done. We have dug deep to find out where these war resisters' families came from, what they experienced, but above all what motivated them and what connected them. We have walked the Bedminster streets and visited the homes, or the sites of homes, of all the war resisters. We have collected census records, marriage and death certificates, newspaper articles, research papers, books etc. Here we set out what we have found out about Bedminster at the beginning of the 20th Century and the 40 local men who have been identified as having refused to fight.

After the Military Service Act introduced conscription in March 1916 all eligible men were deemed to have enlisted in the armed forces. We will see through the stories of some of our Bedminster war resisters, the range of consequences faced by those who, like George Abraham Smith, refused to obey this law, and how they were aided and supported.

This is the hidden history of the Bedminster war resisters.

Part 1 sets the scene, providing a picture of Bedminster in the pre-war and war years 1900–1918. We show the basis for the contention that there was a network of support behind the war resisters. Part 2 details the stories of a dozen of the war resisters and we set out how and why they resisted—either 'Taking a Stand' or 'Going on the Run'. We also show the links between them, which in many cases were political connections. In Part 3 we review the position of the war resisters and their supporters at the end of the war and draw together the evidence for a network of resistance in Bedminster.

Emma Byron & Trevor Houghton–Otherstory, January 2020

Puppetry on the Steps Against War history walk.

Part 1: Setting the scene

Bedminster in the First World War period

The district

Bedminster is a district of Bristol in the south of the city, separated from the centre by the River Avon and the docks. There are three main roads in Bedminster, West Street, North Street and East Street: they join on Cannon Street. The period before the First World War saw the area expand rapidly. It is noticeable that at least five of our war resisters came from families that had moved from the country to the city. New residential areas nearby, such as Southville and Windmill Hill, were built in the decades before the war to provide housing for workers in new industries such as tobacco and printing/packaging. House building itself was a significant source of employment: three of our war resisters were in that trade. St John's Lane to the South and what is now Duckmoor Road to the West were effectively the boundaries of the City. To the south was farmland and to the west was a semi-industrialised landscape including the South Liberty Lane Colliery.

Bedminster was rising from a grim past. During the Victorian period it was known for slum housing, squalor, crime and disease. Growing affluence and new infrastructure saw this change. The main streets became lined with shops, making Bedminster a busy hub for retailing in Bristol[1]. Nine of the war resisters living in the area worked at or in some cases ran shops.

A working-class district

Bedminster was in the 1900s and remained until the 1970s a predominantly working-class area of Bristol. This is reflected in the social mix of our war resisters, with a number doing manual labour of one kind or another. The new industries in the area employed many skilled workers so we see a significant number of printers, machinists and craftsmen. The growth of office work provided clerical jobs for five of the war resisters, two others were in occupations that could be regarded as middle class, one a lecturer and the other a dentist.

1 Bantock A, *Bedminster,* 2001
https://www.bafhs.org.uk/bafhs-parishes/other-bafhs-parishes/52-bedminster

The former Bedminster Town Hall on Cannon Street became Bristol's second picture house in 1909.

At this time, the majority of working-class people would have been living in rented homes. Home ownership was confined to the more affluent and rented housing was almost entirely from private landlords (as mass Council owned rented housing only started following the war).[2] The level of rents was a key social issue and was a subject of campaigning by many of the political groups discussed later. People often took in lodgers to help cover their rent and several of the younger war resisters were lodgers or lived with their employers. As an example, Ernest Harding, who worked as a baker, lived with his employer Ernest Knight over the shop in Essex Street.

Cinemas and music halls

New forms of entertainments emerged. The former Bedminster Town Hall on Cannon Street became Bristol's second picture house in 1909. Viewing films was a hugely popular activity. Early newsreels were shown, providing audiences with a totally novel and vivid view of the world. In August and September 1916 crowds flocked to the screenings of the film *The Battle of*

2 Forbes T & Byrne E, *Homes for Heroes 100—One Hundred Years of Council Housing in Bristol*, (Bristol 2019).

the *Somme*[3]. This provided many people with their first impressions of the horrors of trench warfare as faced by their fathers, sons and brothers, at a time when conscription was really beginning to bite.

Music halls were also a major form of mass entertainment. In 1911 the 2000-seater *Bedminster Hippodrome* opened on East Street. Music halls were widely used as recruiting venues for the armed forces, but their acts also satirised the establishment and kicked back at government controls over ordinary life. Examples of songs from the war period include *Lloyd George's Beer* which poked fun at the introduction of weak government beer (a measure to reduce the food resources going into brewing)[4] and *The Military Representative*, which comically portrayed an officer refusing to exempt anyone from military service, even if they were 91 years old, or already dead![5]

Major industries

Bedminster had a long involvement in the production of leather and despite the decline in the industry there were still several tanneries and cattle yards in the area when the First World War broke out. It would have given a very distinctive odour to the district. One of our war resisters, Frank Pope (74 Beauley Road), had worked at one of these tanneries as a leather roller.

W.D. and H.O. Wills built their first tobacco factory on the site of a former tannery on East Street in the 1880s. In 1901, in response to strong competition from the USA, Wills combined with other tobacco companies to form Imperial Tobacco. In the 1900s a second tobacco factory was built on Raleigh Road /North Street. Hundreds of Bedminster people worked at these factories, as did four of our war resisters. A further six war resister households had family members employed at Wills.

Just off the junction between West Street and East Street were the tram sheds and the Robinson paper bag factory. E.S. & A. Robinson were major manufacturers of cardboard box packaging, paper bags, calendars and almanacs. They were at the forefront of new developments in offset-litho printing and photo-litho printing. Already a major employer in Bedminster, in 1912 they completed a second factory just off West Street on the former site of the Malago Colliery.[6] Just a short walk beyond

3 https://www.iwm.org.uk/history/geoffrey-malins-and-the-battle-of-the-somme-film.
4 *Lloyd George's beer*, Composed by R P Weston and Bert Lee (Francis Day & Hunter: 1915).
5 Mullen J, *Wartime Popular Music*, https://www.bl.uk/world-war-one/articles/wartime-popular-music.
6 Darwin B, *Robinsons of Bristol, 1844–1944*, (Bristol: 1945).

W.D. & H.O. Wills tobacco factory on East Street.

Bedminster, at Temple Gate, Mardon, Son & Hall had their Caxton printing works, which was part of Imperial Tobacco. They produced printed cigarette cards. Seven of our war resisters were printers, of whom we know three were trade unionists.

Going down West Street led to the brick works, coal mines and associated supporting industries. In the early 1900s Bedminster was still an active coal mining area, despite the closure of some of the south Bristol mines such as the one at Dean Lane (shut down in 1906). The main working pit during the First World War was on South Liberty Lane to the west of the district. The steady supply of coal was vital to the war effort. A couple of our war resisters ended up working in mines as 'Work of National Importance' as an alternative to going to fight.

The military in Bedminster: 'Bristol's Own'

The Bristol International Exhibition was held in 1914 on Ashton Meadows beside the river on the edge of Bedminster. It was a kind of theme park and was not entirely a success, closing down in August 1914 just after the outbreak of war. The site became known as *The White City* and was taken over by the military to house the 12th Battalion of the Gloucestershire Regiment.[7] In the opening months of the war 1,300 Bristol men volunteered and were enlisted into the 12th Battalion, which became known as 'Bristol's Own'. On Sundays during 1914/15, they would parade to church down North Street. In November 1915 they were sent to France. Tragically, by the end of the war over half were dead. In October 1918 the Battalion was disbanded.

By the time conscription was introduced in March 1916, it was a rare thing to see a young man on the streets who was not in uniform. Some

7 Burlton C, *Bristol's Lost City: Built to Inspire, Transformed for War.* (Bristol Books: 2014).

Banner depicting 'Bristol's Own' 12th Battalion of the Gloucestershire Regiment - from the Steps Against War history walk.

of those doing 'Work of National Importance' were given a special badge to wear (often by their employers) so that they would not be challenged by members of the public as shirkers from military service.[8] In such circumstances it was hard for conscientious objectors and war resisters to remain invisible.

The political scene in Bedminster and Bristol

Socialism, temperance and nonconformism

In 1900, Gertrude Dix published her novel the *Image Breakers*. This is the story of two 'new women', Rosalind Dangerfield and Leslie Ardent, and their involvement in left politics, set in part in a fictional place called 'Burminster'. Sheila Rowbotham comments on this novel:

> Gertrude situates her plot in recognisable places, evoking milieus and people familiar to her. 'Burminster' borrows from Bedminster, a working-class suburb in Bristol.

8 Read F, 2018 *https://www.iwm.org.uk/history/on-war-service-badge.*

Bedminster Bridge, 1908 postcard.

> Rosalind, troubled by social inequality, starts a class for young working-class women in 'Burminster'...She becomes active in the socialist movement.[9]

This fictional reference shows Bedminster had an active socialist community at the beginning of the 20th Century. In reality this, indeed, was the case.

In these early days of socialism, the Bristol Socialist Society was an unaligned umbrella organisation where people with socialist and anarchist leanings met up, exchanged ideas and together took action. The Society was a vehicle for radical ideas and was strongly anti-liberal. At the turn of the century, there was an active local group of the society in Bedminster and this was instrumental in putting up socialist candidates at elections to the East and West Bedminster Boards of Guardians, who were responsible for providing poor relief.[10] In 1904 William Baster won the council seat of Bedminster East as a socialist.[11] The Bristol Socialist Society continued to be influential right through the pre-war period.

9 Rowbotham, S. *Rebel Crossings—New Women, Free Lovers, and Radicals in Britain and the United States*, (Verso, London, 2016) pp. 284–289.
10 Bryher S, *An Account of the Labour and Socialist Movement in Bristol,* (Bristol 1931) p. 162.
11 Richardson M, *Bristol and the Labour Unrest of 1910–14,* (BRHG 2013) p 12.

Another umbrella for the left in the pre-war years was *The Clarion*. This was a populist socialist newspaper published by Robert Blatchford. A whole range of social clubs became associated with the newspaper:

> In addition to cycling, which gained the biggest following, the main activities before the First World War were choral singing and rambling (the latter combined with nature-study). All the activities were, to a greater or lesser extent, connected with Socialist propaganda work. And they tended to overlap, so that cyclists, choirs and ramblers often met up at the same Saturday or Sunday afternoon venue.[12]

The Clarion carried reports of the activities of the Clarion clubs: for example, this report from 9th June 1911 about the Clarion Vocal Union in Bristol (with a mention of Bedminster war resister Fred Berriman):

> BRISTOL, Conductor, Mr Harry Begbie, 63 St. Michael's Hill; secretary, Mr Fred Berriman, 19 Hall Street, Bedminster...with a party of 25 won first prize in the Bedminster Eisteddfod. Test piece, Sullivan's "The Long Day Closes". Our first attempt at competition work.

The Clarion Cycle Clubs were particularly popular, and leisure was always combined with propagandising:

> It is said that in the twenty years before the First World War a Clarion cyclist, almost by definition, was someone riding a machine with saddlebag crammed or carrier piled high with copies of the paper, all of which would eventually be sold or given away.[13]

There were a couple of Clarion Cycle Clubs in Bristol and as the listings in the Clarion demonstrate, Bedminster Bridge was a regular place to meet when there was a club ride. Given that we have two politically involved bicycle shop proprietors (George Barker and Walter Told) in the group of Bedminster war resisters it seems very likely they would have been part of these activities along with other keen cyclists.

12 Working Class Movement Library, https://www.wcml.org.uk/our-collections/creativity-and-culture.
13 Working Class Movement Library, https://www.wcml.org.uk/our-collections/creativity-and-culture.

There were a number of Clarion Vans around the country. These were horse drawn caravans which would be used for the distribution of socialist literature and copies of the Clarion, on tours led by women. The 17th March 1911 edition of the Clarion shows the planned route for one such Clarion Van around Bristol, on May 16th & 17th, listing all the stops including Bedminster. It was the practice for members of the Clarion cycle clubs to meet up with vans and help to hand out literature.[14]

Robert Blatchford (publisher and owner of the *Clarion*) took a pro-war stance and this was reflected in the articles in the paper. On 22nd January 1915 in a front-page article titled: *A Cheap and Nasty Conscription*, Blatchford criticised proposals for the introduction of conscription. However, he advocated conscription on 'British lines' implying a more liberal/flexible approach rather than an authoritarian 'Prussian' imposition of conscription. His support for conscription alienated many of his readers and the paper's circulation plummeted, but support for the clubs and particularly the cycling clubs held up.

Another feature of the pre-war period was temperance. In his description of the Bristol temperance movement, Alan Clarke reports that the 1906 edition of the *Bristol Temperance Federation Record* lists no less than 97 local societies with almost half claiming membership over 100.[15] There was a considerable overlap between nonconformist Christians (Baptists, Methodists, Quakers etc), the membership of the temperance societies, and membership of socialist groups including the Independent Labour Party (ILP) and the British Socialist Party (BSP). This is demonstrated by the use of the Temperance Hall on Bedminster Parade as a venue for meetings of the Bedminster Ward of the ILP and the Bristol branch of the BSP.[16] The popularity of temperance led to the establishment of coffee taverns, as an alternative to pubs, as places to socialise; they were also more welcoming to women. Alan Clarke records that at the turn of the century in the commercial directories there were eight coffee taverns listed in Bedminster. In Gertude Dix's novel, *The Image Breakers,* a lead character, Leslie Ardent, visited coffee taverns in pursuit of anarchist and socialist ideas.[17]

---

14 Pye D, *Fellowship is Life—The National Clarion Cycling Club 1895–1995*, (Clarion Publishing, Bolton 1995) pp. 36 – 37.

15 Clarke A, *Taking the Pledge: the Temperance Movement in Bristol, 1830–1914*, (Avon Local History and Archaeology, Bristol 2019) p. 32.

16 *Labour Leader* 5th May 1911; *Clarion* 12th Jan 1912.

17 There appears to have been a decline in the number of coffee taverns in Bedminster immediately before the war with some becoming luncheon bars and refreshment rooms. The Temperance Hall on Bedminster Parade was demolished in March 1913 to make way for a new public library.

Loxton drawing: The Temperance Hall on Bedminster Parade.

In 1898, following the example of socialists in Scotland, the Bristol Socialist Society launched a venture amongst the young: a Socialist Sunday School. This initially took a very Christian model for educating young people about socialism, as activities would include singing and hearing a 'lesson'. It went through a few iterations during the pre-war years. It met first at the Sheppards Hall in Old Market and then in rooms facing the Horsefair, rented to the Bristol Socialist Society and known as The Socialist Centre. These early efforts paved the way for the Independent Labour Party's successful Socialist Sunday School at the Kingsley Hall, Old Market, after 1911.[18] We will see later that some of the Bedminster war resisters (the Chappells and William Livingston) were involved in this Sunday School that drew in people from a range of socialist groups, including the Socialist Labour Party.

As the war began in 1914, and concerns grew that the government might introduce conscription, Christian pacifists and some left groups came together to form the No-Conscription Fellowship. It was founded in London on 27th November 1914, as proposed by Lilla Brockway[19] and had affiliated groups around the country, including Bristol. The focus of the campaign was opposing conscription and later supporting conscientious objectors. Annie Chappell (25 Kensal Road) was Bristol branch secretary.

18 Bryher, *An Account of the Labour & Socialist Movement,* pp. 146–147.
19 Brockway F, *Inside Left: Thirty Years of Platform, Press, Prison and Parliament* (New Leader: 1942) pp. 66–67.

Left groups

At the beginning of the 20th century there was some fluidity in people's affiliation to particular left groups, particularly prior to the Bolshevik revolution in Russia in October 1917. For many their socialist beliefs had a strong connection to their Christian faith. Whether to support or oppose the war was an issue that did divide left political groups and trade unionists. The ILP took a strong anti-war stance but the Labour Party was part of the Coalition Government who were prosecuting the war. The British Socialist Party split over their position on the war. Nonetheless there was a significant section of left-wing activists, including those in the Socialist Labour Party and anarchists, who were strongly opposed to the war.

The Independent Labour Party (ILP)

The ILP was one of the main socialist groups in the UK at the time, and one of its largest branches was in Bristol. It aimed to further independent working-class politics through an alliance with the growing trade union movement. The ILP (like the Bristol Socialist Society) was committed to achieving change through the ballot box and greater state intervention.[20] Many ILP members were campaigners for women's suffrage. The ILP held a central place in resistance to the war and its national paper *The Labour Leader* was an important outlet for anti-war opinion. It was very active in the No-Conscription Fellowship. While it was affiliated to the Labour Party and worked within it to put up 'Labour' candidates at elections it remained independently to the left, particularly in its stance towards the war. A key Bedminster war resister, Fred Berriman (19 Hall Street), was at various times chairman and secretary of the Bristol Branch of the ILP.

Socialist Labour Party (SLP)

As we will see later, the SLP, a Marxist group, also had a presence in Bedminster. Bert Chappell (25 Kensal Road), another war resister, was the Secretary of the Bristol branch. The SLP advocated direct action by workers as a route to political change, though they did also stand as candidates in elections. They were committed to militant industrial unionism with a focus on grassroots organising, and to political education:

20 Hannam J, *Bristol Independent Labour Party*, (BRHG 2014) pp. 5–10.

forming study groups and producing affordable editions of socialist classics (e.g. a translation of the Communist Manifesto, sold for a penny).[21] They opposed the war from the start, declaring in their paper, *The Socialist*, 'Our position is neither pro-German nor pro-British, but anti-capitalist ... The capitalist classes of all nations are our real enemies, and it is against them that we direct our attack.'[22] The Bristol branch was active in networking and agitating beyond Bristol.[23]

The Party had branches around the country, though most were in Scotland (its HQ was in Glasgow), and the North of England. It was small, but its members were active in maintaining its networks and its links with other groups, travelling often. It was very supportive of the Irish republican movement; James Connolly, the radical Irish nationalist and trade union leader, had been a founding member of the SLP during his time in Scotland, and maintained close links with the party until his execution in 1916.

As Sheila Rowbotham describes, Connolly's influence on SLP political thinking provided a counter to its often-strict adherence to a party line: his 'critique of an omniscient party allowed for much greater autonomy for rank and file workers' groups and for social movements', including nationalist rebellion and women's emancipation. Socialists could support and learn from the diverse struggles of oppressed groups. As well as supporting Irish republicans in print via *The Socialist*, the SLP secretly printed Connolly's paper *The Irish Worker* when it was banned in Ireland in 1915; Scottish SLP members smuggled it to Dublin, where they met members of Connolly's Irish Citizen Army.[24]

Anarchists

Anarchists were among the activists organising in Bristol, whether as named groups, or in looser networks. A Bristol Anarchist Group is recorded in 1913 as one of a number of local groups affirming their support for women's suffrage.[25] A Bristol branch of the anarchist-communist Workers' Freedom Group was based in The Haymarket, the area in the

---

21 Challinor R, *John S. Clarke*, (Pluto 1977) pp. 22–3.
22 Ibid p. 38.
23 Socialists Mobbed, *Western Gazette* 6th October 1911: 'Scenes of a lively character were witnessed in the town [Yeovil] on Sunday evening arising out of an open are meeting held under the auspices of the Socialist Labour Party...[it] was addressed by a "comrade" from Bristol, named G.E.Barker...'.
24 Rowbotham S, *Friends of Alice Wheeldon*, (Pluto 2015), pp. 17–18.
25 The Feeling in the Country, *Votes for Women*, 25th April 1913.

city centre where Walter Lewis and others made political speeches.[26] The Workers' Freedom Groups had been set up in 1913 in Wales and parts of England out of resentment among workers—especially miners—at the behaviour of union leaders during the industrial unrest of the pre-war years.[27] The groups set up discussion circles and reading rooms, and produced propaganda promoting industrial unionism, and opposing the war and conscription.[28]

In 1915 the Bristol group published *The Last War*, a pamphlet by the anarchist and former Bristolian George Barrett:

> Let us leave it to the bomb-throwers and warlords to proclaim their love of peace...to the Christians and their churches who have pronounced their blessing on the war, to boast of their humility and their habit of turning the other cheek ... It is war we proclaim, the last war, the international war in which the workers of all lands shall be united against the invaders—the rich who have seized the land and lived on the labour of the poor.[29]

More broadly, anarchist values and approaches were reflected in the activity of Clarion Clubs in the area (mostly before the war). Denis Pye states, 'The Clarion movement in its first two decades can be seen as an attempt to pre-figure life under socialism as William Morris had seen it'[30]—that is, a libertarian socialism with a close kinship to anarchism. While avowedly socialist, it was not affiliated to a particular party, and involved leftists of all kinds. Its tendency to decentralised organising and free association, with some flyposting thrown in, has an anarchist flavour. In 1914, the National Clarion Cycling Clubs' objectives were 'Mutual aid, good fellowship and the propagation of Socialism as advocated by the Clarion'[31]—which, as Steve Hunt notes, references Kropotkin as well as Morris.[32]

---

26 The group were based at 19 the Haymarket: this was also the address of Jack Flynn's radical bookshop, sometimes known as the "Bomb Shop". Hunt S, *Anarchism in Bristol and the West Country*, (BRHG 2010) p. 27; Wrights Directory 1913.
27 Quail J, *The Slow Burning Fuse: The Lost History of the British Anarchists*, (1978), pp. 278–9. Quail references a grassroots anarchism in the miners' movement in South Wales—which likely was an influence for some Bristol activists.
28 Heath N, *Anarchists Against World War 1*, 2013, https://libcom.org/history/anarchists-against-world-war-one-two-little-known-events-abertillery-stockport; Quail, *The Slow Burning Fuse*, p. 278.
29 McKay I, Ed. *Our Masters are Helpless: The Essays of George Barrett*, (Freedom Press 2019), p39; Hunt S, *Anarchism in Bristol...*, p. 27.
30 Pye D, *Fellowship is Life*, p. 48.
31 Ibid. p. 26.
32 Hunt, *Anarchism in..*, p78.

We will see that some Bedminster war resisters had anarchist leanings and connections. George Barker (12 Cannon Street) was labelled by the security services as an anarchist. William Livingston (45 Vicarage Road) relied on his relationship with a group of anarchists from London to try to evade capture while on the run from conscription.

Meeting places

In Bedminster, from 1913, the Independent Labour Party (ILP) held its monthly ward meetings in the East Street Co-operative Hall and was actively propagandising on the streets.[33] During the war years (and before) the ILP's Bristol headquarters at the Kingsley Hall in Old Market was the venue for Bristol-wide meetings of a whole range of left-wing groups and trade unions. So this was a place where many of the Bedminster war resisters would have met up, got to know each other, and debated tactics. They would also have attended public meetings there, where they would learn about the resistance to the war in other parts of the UK and internationally.

Other political meeting points were the places where activists addressed a wider public. Bedminster Bridge, Victoria Park and outside the London Inn were local venues for open air meetings.[34] Elsewhere in Bristol, key places were Eastville Park, where ILP Chairman Fred Berriman addressed the crowds[35], the Haymarket in the centre of Bristol, where Bedminster war resister Walter Lewis, a tobacco worker, was arrested, and Durdham Downs where Bedminster absentee Sidney Vicary Vowles would take his soap box. So some of the Bedminster war resisters were individuals who would be recognised by the general populace as actively opposed to the war.

National links, political and underground networks

The political links of the Bedminster war resisters stretched well beyond the city. In Fred Berriman, Annie and Bert Chappell, Bedminster had left-wing leading figures in Bristol who also represented the city's socialists at national political gatherings. William Livingston's experiences also show him as an individual with national connections. George Barker and his wife Minnie May had links with Whiteway, an anarchist colony near Stroud.[36]

33 *Labour Leader* 22nd September 1915.
34 *Labour Leader* 9th May 1911 & 29th May 1913.
35 *Labour Leader* 12th August 1915.
36 Breeden P, 'It wasn't all God Save the King when war broke out', *South Bristol Voice,* December 2018 pp. 36–40. Breeden states that the Barkers went to live at Whiteway in the 1920s.

Whiteway was a refuge for some objectors on the run, and runaways may have moved between there and the secret chamber created by George in Bedminster—of which more later.

Close to Bedminster, the City Docks offered possibilities for escape by sea. Arthur Horner, a miner and union leader from South Wales, was helped by war resisters in Bristol to evade conscription by travelling to Ireland: 'I went from Abertillery to Bristol and there with the help of sympathisers fixed up the crossing to Dublin ... There I enlisted in the Irish Citizen Army'.[37] We don't know who helped him: the SLP with its Irish Republican sympathies, and the Workers' Freedom Group with its connections to Welsh miners, are possibilities, as are ILP members with links to dockside unions. After the war Horner would become a colleague of Bedminster activist Annie Chappell, when both were active in the Communist Party in South Wales.

Arthur Horner, miner and union leader from South Wales.

So we can see that in the pre-war period, in Bedminster and beyond, there was a rich social network and range of meeting points for political activists that was to spawn our group of Bedminster war resisters. This political network was also what sustained the war resisters after conscription was introduced in 1916.

Labour militancy

The years before the war saw an increase in labour militancy in Bristol with a number of major strikes, particularly on the docks, railways, trams, mines and in the building trade. These disputes manifested themselves in Bedminster in various ways.

37 Horner A, *Incorrigible Rebel*, (London, MacGibbon and Kee 1960) pp. 28–29.

For example, Bedminster people were active in August 1911 during the National Rail Strike. Newspaper reports show them pulling over lorries attempting to carry goods from the railway good yards at Temple Meads, including those carrying materials to the Wills cigarette factory.[38] On 19th August, an angry crowd surrounded and threw stones at a signal box at the Portishead Junction on the edge of Bedminster. They wanted to force a signalman strike-breaker to stop work. A company of soldiers were called to the scene and fired warning shots over the heads of the crowd. When the police arrived, they charged the crowd with batons and dispersed them. One of the crowd, Joseph Parker, was later taken to hospital unconscious after receiving a blow to the head.[39]

In 1912 the National Miners' Strike had a strong local impact. Around 2,500 miners in Bristol rallied behind the strike call and a prolonged dispute ensued. The strike caused great hardship for the families and particularly the children of the miners. In Bedminster, the Salvation Army on Dean Lane supplied hundreds of breakfasts daily for hungry children who devoured cocoa, bread and butter ('and not a crumb was left').[40]

Bedminster's two biggest employers, Wills and Robinson's, could be typified as paternalistic in their management style.[41] The employees of the two companies were relatively well paid—and neither was directly involved in strikes during this period. Among our war resisters were at least three members of print unions: Fred Berriman was the President of the Bristol Typographical Society, Albert Chappell was a member of the National Union of Printers and Paper Workers, and Henry Williams was a member of the Amalgamated Society of Lithographic Printers.[42] They were part of the skilled 'aristocracy' of the trade union movement.

Though the print workers did not take a direct part in the militancy of the period they can still be seen to be acting collectively in solidarity with other workers. In June 1913 Robinson's Litho. Dept. was listed as contributing £1 1s to the 'Black Country Fund' in the *Daily Herald*. This was in support of a major and successful strike by engineering workers for a 23s minimum wage for unskilled workers. The strike lasted two months, with over 40,000 workers coming out in support. It jeopardised the government's armaments programme during the Anglo-German naval arms race that preceded the war.[43] It is notable that this group of skilled

38 *Bristol Times and Mirror* 11th August 1911.
39 *Bristol Times and Mirror* 21st August 1911.
40 Richardson M. *Bristol and the Labour Unrest,* p. 33.
41 Richardson M. *Trade Unionism and Industrial Conflict* http://humanities.uwe.ac.uk/bhr/Main/.
42 Britain, Trade Union Membership Registers https://search.findmypast.co.uk/.
43 *Daily Herald* 26th June 1913.

The Robinson building, Bedminster in present times.

Loxton drawing: Bedminster Hippodrome, a 2,000-seat music hall on East Street.

lithographers gave their support to the rights of unskilled workers. The *Daily Herald* (31st October 1915) also reported on resolutions being passed by various groups in support of the release of the trade unionist and Irish republican Jim Larkin from Mountjoy Prison following his pivotal role in the 'Dublin lockout'[44]. Among these were 'the Litho Society at Robinson's Bedminster works' which probably included Henry Williams (Clifton Terrace).

In the spring of 1914, a prolonged lockout of tramway workers sparked solidarity actions across the city. In Bedminster 100 men downed tools at Mullett's Motor Body works on York Road because they were not prepared to do work sent from the Bristol Tramway Company. After gaining assurances from their management that Mullett's would not undertake any work from the Tramway Company, they went back to work.[45]

During the summer of 1914, building workers were on strike in Bristol for better pay. Two of our war resisters, Ernest Roe and George Abraham Smith, were members of the Amalgamated Society of Carpenters and Joiners and another, Arthur Mason, was a building labourer. The *Western Daily Press* (18th July 1914) reported that: '...a successful variety entertainment took place at the Bedminster Hippodrome on Thursday evening under the auspices of the Joint Strike Committee'. The artists performed for free for the benefit of the striking brick layers and building labourers. Phil Melton, a popular comedian, sang *Two Bob an Hour* and performed a burlesque, *Don't go down the mine.*

In August 1914, as the possibility of war became imminent, some Bristol trade unionists did collectively express their opposition to war. On Sunday 2nd August, Bristol dockers held a mass meeting on the waterfront. At this moment of crisis, the members of the dockers' union and their leaders came together in public to debate whether the union should support the drive to war or not.

Ernest Bevin, organiser for the dockers' union, spoke: he said that 'English Trade Unionists are on the most friendly terms with Trade Unionists across the Continent. It would be insane to fight them simply because there is a dispute between Austria and Serbia'. He proposed a resolution: 'that this meeting of organised workers calls on the Government to immediately declare its neutrality in connection with the European war;

44 This started with Dublin United Tramway Company sacking workers who had joined the Irish Transport and General Workers' Union (started by Larkin). The dispute rapidly spread with other employers locking out or sacking ITGWU members to become one of the most serious industrial disputes in Ireland's history, involving thousands of workers and lasting 7 months.
45 *Daily Herald* 14th April 1914.

View down West Street with the tram depot at the end 1913.

and on the TUC and the Labour Party to call a national conference to discuss ways to prevent this country from being involved in "hostilities". [46]

The motion was passed unanimously. Later that same day an anti-war demonstration was held on the Downs. The next day, at an emergency meeting, the National Railway Women's Guild and the Bristol branch of the National Union of Railwaymen also passed resolutions for peace—as they said they had no quarrel with their fellow workers on the continent.[47]

The coming of the war did not see an end to labour militancy. In January 1916, the Carpenters' Union and the NUR, at one of a series of joint meetings in Bristol between the Trades Council and Labour Representation Committee, advocated the use of strikes against conscription.[48] By 1917/18 war weariness and the influence of the Russian revolutions prompted a resurgence in labour unrest.

During the war women had taken on many roles previously filled by men, but seldom for the same pay. In August 1918 women tram and bus workers struck for equal pay, the strike beginning in London but spreading

46 Ball R. *Should Britain Go to War with Germany?* https://www.brh.org.uk/site/articles/britain-go-war-germany/ 2014.
47 Ibid.
48 Hannam, *Bristol Independent Labour Party*, pp. 30–32.

to other cities including Bristol. [49] Bedminster had its own tram depot (at the junction of West Street and East Street) with tram and bus routes running along all its main streets. In the period of the strike at the end of August 1918 these streets were devoid of trams and buses.[50] Male tram workers supported the strike. One of our war resisters, Sidney Sprague (14 Elmdale Road), was a tram driver. The women won a 5-shilling bonus, but not equal pay.

These events show that the working people of Bedminster were willing to stand up for themselves and were resilient to the privations that followed from going on strike. Labour militancy both before and during the First World War was part of the political context in which some Bedminster residents mounted their resistance to the war.

49 Weller K, *Don't be a soldier!* 1985 p 32–33 https://libcom.org/history/dont-be-soldier-radical-anti-war-movement-north-london-1914-1918-ken-weller.
50 *Western Daily Press* 20th August 1918.

THE

MILITARY SERVICE ACT, 1916

Applies to **Unmarried Men** who, on August 15th, 1915, were 18 years of age or over and who will not be 41 years of age on March 2nd, 1916.

ALL MEN, NOT EXCEPTED OR EXEMPTED, between these ages who on November 2nd, 1915, were unmarried or widowers without any child dependent on them will on

THURSDAY, MARCH 2nd, 1916,

Be deemed to be Enlisted for the Period of the War.

THEY WILL BE PLACED IN THE RESERVE UNTIL CALLED UP IN THEIR CLASS.

MEN EXCEPTED :

SOLDIERS, including Territorials who have volunteered for Foreign Service ;

MEN serving in the **NAVY** or **ROYAL MARINES**;

MEN **DISCHARGED FROM ARMY OR NAVY**, disabled or ill, or **TIME-EXPIRED MEN** ;

MEN REJECTED for the Army since August 14th, 1915;

CLERGYMEN, PRIESTS and MINISTERS OF RELIGION ; VISITORS from the DOMINIONS.

Men who may be exempted by Local Tribunals :

Men more useful to the Nation in their present employments ;

Men in whose case Military Service would cause serious hardship owing to exceptional financial or business obligations or domestic position;

Men who are ill or infirm ;

Men who conscientiously object to combatant service. If the Tribunal thinks fit, men may, on this ground, be (a) exempted from combatant service only (not non-combatant service), or (b) exempted on condition that they are engaged in work of National importance.

Up to March 2nd, a man can apply to his Local Tribunal for a certificate of exemption. There is a Right of Appeal. He will not be called up until his case has been dealt with finally.

Certificates of exemption may be absolute, conditional or temporary. Such certificates can be renewed, varied or withdrawn.

Men retain their Civil Rights until called up and are amenable to Civil Courts only.

DO NOT WAIT UNTIL MARCH 2nd.
ENLIST VOLUNTARILY NOW

For fuller particulars of the Act, please apply for Leaflet No. 64 to the nearest Post Office, Police Station, or Recruiting Office.

Published by the Parliamentary Recruiting Committee, London.   Poster No. 154.   The Abbey Press. Westminster, S.W.

Military Service Act 1916, official WW1 poster.

Part 2: The resisters

Confronting the system

Most of the men resisting conscription faced a common process which started with claiming exemption from combatant service on conscience or other grounds, as provided for by the Military Service Act 1916. They did this at a Military Service Tribunal. Nearly all the Bedminster men who refused to fight appeared before a tribunal at some point, most in Bristol but others at places near to where they were imprisoned. As we will see, the degree to which individuals co-operated with the Tribunal process and accepted decisions varied.

The Joint Advisory Committee for Conscientious Objectors brought together people from a range of political and religious groups. A key member group was the Bristol No-Conscription Fellowship. The Committee's members provided advice and support for conscientious objectors (COs) before they appeared at a tribunal, and wrote to and visited them in prison. They gave support to their families, and published leaflets to raise public awareness.

From March to August 1916 the Bristol Military Service Tribunal, held in what is now the Registry Office in Corn Street, processed hundreds of cases of men seeking exemption. Where we know the dates, we can see that ten of the Bedminster COs appeared before the tribunals in March, seven in April, five in July, one in June and two in August. On 4th August 1916 the *Western Daily Press* reported that the Bristol Tribunal had nearly completed all the first claims for exemption. Hearings did continue till the end of the war but with a much lower number of applicants.

The tribunals were public hearings, and family and friends frequently supported those appearing. Also present were supporters from the Joint Advisory Committee for Conscientious Objectors[1] and representatives of groups such as the ILP, which reported the events in its paper *Bristol Forward*. On 14th March, the *Western Daily Press* reported in an article headed: *Appeals by 150 Single Men—Big Batch of Conscientious Objectors*,

> The public—or rather that portion of the public antagonistic to the national endeavour to preserve the integrity of our empire—attended in larger numbers than on any previous occasion, and the applicants for exemption found themselves in a decidedly sympathetic atmosphere.

1 BRHG, *Refusing to Kill—Bristol's World War 1 Conscientious Objectors*, (BRHG 2019) p. 17.

At least two Bedminster men were at this particular hearing. These early tribunals might be compared to the Magistrates Court hearings in 1990 when hundreds of people who refused to pay their poll tax were summoned and the courts were transformed into a place of protest. As a result, the Military Service Tribunals were a place where both conscientious objectors (COs) and their supporters would have met up and could have formed more lasting links where these did not already exist.

Very few men were granted absolute exemption. Some got temporary exemption on the basis that they were needed by their employers or were already doing 'Work of National Importance'—such as George Barker, cycle shop proprietor (12 Cannon Street). Most who claimed exemption on conscience grounds were told to either take up 'Work of National Importance' such as Gilbert Silverthorn (52 North Street) or to report to the Non-Combatant Corps. Several of the Bedminster War Resisters were given this choice and refused to comply—such as Ernest Rudman (25 Kensal Road). As a result, they were usually arrested as absentees, taken before a magistrate and fined, then handed over to a military barracks. This was often Horfield Barracks, though some Bedminster men were sent to Worcester Barracks. They would then face a court martial followed by imprisonment or a Home Office work camp. Many faced a repeating cycle of imprisonment, as Lois Bibbings notes: "[O]nce their sentences were completed these men were handed back to the military and, consequently, their continued disobedience could result in further court martials and periods of incarceration".[2] Some men went on the run before being arrested e.g. Walter Told (62 North Street)—of which more later.

The Policeman in their midst—Detective Constable Woods

Herbert Charles Woods came to Bristol from South Wales. We first see him in the 1901 Census as Constable Woods, aged 23, living as a boarder at 13 Algiers Street on Windmill Hill, Bedminster. The 1911 Census records that he was married with five children and living at 27 Paultow Road, Windmill Hill.

His house placed him just a hundred metres from the home of key war resisters Annie and Bert Chappell. Within a quarter of mile were the homes of no less than a dozen other war resisters. He was part of B Division of Bristol Constabulary, based a fifteen-minute walk away at Bedminster Police Station on Bedminster Parade. He was truly a policeman in the midst of the Bedminster anti-war network.

2 Bibbings L, *Telling Tales About Men,* (Manchester University Press 2009) p. 32.

The police and military had a 'catch all' legal framework to tackle anti-war activity. The Defence of the Realm Act (DORA) became law on 8th August 1914, four days after Britain entered the First World War. It was added to throughout the war. DORA gave the government and military sweeping powers to take control of land and resources to prosecute the war. It also allowed the government to create new criminal offences as it saw fit, to help progress the war. It consequently provided the military and the police with a tool to deal with anyone who hindered the war effort, such as those political activists who sought to voice opposition to the war.[3]

DORA was used against those who organised strikes such as the Clydeside workers John MacLean, Willie Gallacher, and John William Muir. When conscription was introduced by the Military Service Act in March 1916, DORA was used to suppress individuals and groups who gave succour to those refusing to fight. Among these were the leaders of the No-Conscription Fellowship including Bertrand Russell and Walter Ayles (a key Bristol war resister) who were jailed for publishing a *Repeal the Act* flyer.[4]

In Bedminster, Detective Constable Woods actively pursued the local anti-war support network as he tried to flush out the deserters and COs who were flouting the Military Service Act.

On 11th January 1916 Detective Woods appeared at the Bristol Police Court having apprehended an 'absentee' or deserter.[5] His zealous enforcement of the Military Service Act is evidenced by numerous further mentions in the court reports of the *Western Daily Press* from March 1916 onwards. He appears as a witness and arresting officer of a young man named Price as the very first conscription cases were heard at the Bristol Police Court on 29th March 1916.[6] He subsequently arrested a number of COs and deserters, including George Abraham Smith of 63 Greville Road,[7] Ernest Rudman of 25 Kensal Road,[8] Thomas Durbin who failed to join his ship,[9] Thomas Clark who worked at the South Liberty Lane Colliery[10] and Henry Moseley, a sailor with the Royal Navy Reserve.[11]

3 Hynes G, *Defence of the Realm Act (DORA)* https://encyclopedia.1914-1918-online.net/article/defence_of_the_realm_act_dora.
4 BRHG, Refusing to Kill p34.
5 *Western Daily Press* 12th January 1916.
6 *Western Daily Press* 30th March 1916.
7 *Western Daily Press* 8th May 1916.
8 *Western Daily Press* 1st November 1916.
9 *Western Daily Press* 30th April 1917.
10 *Western Daily Press* 13th April 1917.
11 *Western Daily Press* 3rd September 1918.

Detective Woods arrests George Abraham Smith, paper theatre from Steps Against War history walk.

Accompanied by Police Constable Dempsey, it was Woods who faced a barrage of bricks thrown by deserter George Wilkins and his mother Alice Harver as they resisted arrest from the roof of their Bedminster Down home in November 1917, as we will see.[12]

At the same time Woods can be seen using DORA against anyone who might have been supporting these deserters and COs. Even seemingly petty infringements under DORA did not escape Woods' attention. For example, Woods arrested Thomas Walter Williamson of 370 Stapleton Road for carrying on a business of receiving letters without notifying the police. He was fined £1.[13]

His most notable arrest was in March 1917, when he apprehended George Barker, the Bedminster cycle shop owner who had excavated a secret chamber to hide COs and deserters. Barker was found guilty under DORA 'with committing an act prejudicial to the Defence of the Realm with intent to assist the enemy'. In this and in several of the other cases listed here, it is clear that Woods worked closely with the military, and that together they kept suspect individuals under surveillance. In

12 *The Illustrated Police Gazette* 29th November 1917.
13 *Western Daily Press* 19th July 1917.

this instance it appears they also had information from the secret agent, William Rickard.

As we will see later, DORA was also used against international socialist Walter Lewis (15 Victoria Place) who was accused of making inflammatory speeches in the centre of Bristol at the Haymarket.

Taking a stand

Many of our resisters took a principled and public stand against conscription, and against the war. They engaged with the legal process that faced them, stating their position at tribunals and in court.

Within these structures, men practised non-cooperation to different degrees. Some, like Gilbert Silverthorn, while refusing to fight, accepted a conditional exemption and took on alternative work. Others, like Fred Berriman, took an absolutist position, refusing to take any work supporting the war, or to obey any military order when taken to barracks.

For many COs, like Berriman, going to prison for their beliefs was an act of collective resistance, and was linked to resistance on the outside. As he wrote after the war,

> War resisters have no memories of the horrors of war or the "brotherhood of the trenches," but they have memories of a glorious fight against militarism and on behalf of the great principle of human brotherhood, for which they have no regrets, a fight that was conducted by the banding together of a few organisations (including the Independent Labour Party and the No-Conscription Fellowship) for the purpose of resisting, in some cases, military service only, and in others both military and alternative service.[14]

Some resisters had campaigned against conscription prior to its introduction, and those who were able continued this work throughout the war, as well as running networks of support for those in prison. We will see the example of Annie Chappell, who ran the Bristol branch of the No-Conscription Fellowship, while her husband Bert and housemate Ernest were among those resisting on the inside.

We will also hear the story of Walter Lewis, who had gained exemption from the tribunals, but continued to speak out publicly against the war, at some risk to his own liberty.

14 Berriman F., Memories of a War Resister, *Labour Weekly* 30th July 1927 p 2.

Annie and Bert Chappell—socialist organisers

Just up the hill from Detective Woods was a household of active resisters at 25 Kensal Road, Windmill Hill. Annie Chappell, who was secretary of the Bristol No-Conscription Fellowship, lived with her husband Bert, a printer, and their friends Ernest and Florence Rudman, tobacco workers. The couples had set up house together some time after they each married in 1912.[15]

Bert was secretary of the Bristol branch of the Socialist Labour Party (SLP), a Marxist group.[16] Annie was very likely involved too, given her later political activity. Ernest was a Methodist: his recorded words suggest Christian Socialist beliefs, more akin to many in the Independent Labour Party, and unlike the atheist Chappells.

Conversations round the table here must have explored and tested these differences, found the common ground. In this it was a household characteristic of the time, where intertwining strands of the left coexisted; and while ideologies might conflict, in practice there was some fluidity and overlap. Sheila Rowbotham describes the "extraordinary creative flux" of the period 1910 to 1919, and the sharing of ideas and tactics between labour, socialist, feminist and peace activists.[17]

The Chappells were also involved with Bristol Socialist Sunday School. Many people involved in the Socialist Sunday School movement saw it as a way to teach socialism through the language of traditional Christian ethics, and values of love and cooperation. Other members brought a more secular approach, with a focus on the social and economic aims of socialism, and a clear analysis of capitalism.[18] This emphasis varied between and within groups. The Chappells were clearly representative of this left wing, and may have been involved as educators, sharing SLP ideas. Meetings were attended by people of all ages, and might include a talk or "lesson", discussion, singing, and a collection for a chosen charity or fund.

At two of its meetings in summer 1915, Bristol Socialist Sunday School raised money for the William Holliday defence fund. The Chappells are listed among the donors by *The Socialist,* the SLP newspaper. [19] Holliday

15 Pearce Register entries for Albert E. Chappell & Ernest Rudman; photo of NCF membership card signed by Annie Chappell; Marriage records for Albert E. Chappell and Annie Warren, Ernest Rudman and Florence S. Coleman; 1911 census entries for Ernest Rudman and for Florence S. Coleman.
16 *Branch Directory, The Socialist*, Jan 1915—via Cyril Pearce.
17 Rowbotham, *Friends of Alice Wheeldon*, p. 39.
18 Reid F, Socialist Sunday Schools, *International Review of Social History* Vol. 11, No. 1 (1966), p. 33
19 Wm. Holliday Defence Fund, *The Socialist*, July 1915; Pearce Register entry for Albert Chappell.

Bert Chappell and Ernest Rudman, rod puppets from Steps Against War history walk.

was a member of the SLP and the Industrial Workers of the World (IWW), who had been sentenced to three months hard labour under DORA. He had made a speech in Birmingham's Bull Ring, at which he 'denounced the attacks which have been made on Germans...living in this country, and justified his defence of persecuted aliens by reminding the audience that the King is a German.'[20] A diverse range of socialist and labour movement groups came together in solidarity with Holliday, raising funds that enabled him to appeal his conviction.[21]

With the start of conscription, Bert Chappell and Ernest Rudman would themselves be in need of solidarity. As married men, they became eligible for military service in May 1916.

A tobacco cutter, probably Ernest, at a Military Service Tribunal in July, said that 'if the tribunal wished to know his views they should apply to his newsagent, who would tell them the kind of literature he read. This, he said would be better evidence than letters from half a dozen parsons.'

20 Savage Sentence under Defence of the Realm Act, *Labour Leader*, 3rd June 1915.
21 Holliday's appeal was successful, but later that year he was jailed again, and died while in prison. A memorial event for him was held in Birmingham's Bull Ring, with speeches by Willie Paul and Bristol SLP and Socialist Sunday School member James Stewart. Conviction Quashed, *Birmingham Daily Post*, 6th July 1915; Pearce C, *Communities of Resistance: Patterns of Dissent in Britain, 1914–1918* (Francis Boutle, 2020 Forthcoming); Socialist Labour Party listing, Labour Leader, 25th May 1916.

CHAPPELL, A.—Was refused all exemption, and arrested on military warrant without being taken to the police court. He was serving his second sentence in Exeter Gaol, but was suddenly recalled to his unit at Fort Tregantle, Devonport, where no civilian may enter to see him.

Extract from What Every Bristol Man Should Know, leaflet published by the Joint Advisory Committee for Conscientious Objectors 1917.

Asked what he read, he replied 'Tolstoy, Ruskin and Carlyle'—a list that suggests ideas of Christian pacifism, ethical socialism and the importance of individual conscience. He claimed that 'as a productive unit of society he was doing work of national importance, and he declined to take any other'. He was ordered to find 'Work of National Importance' within two weeks.[22]

He seems not to have done so, as in late October he was arrested at home by his near neighbour Detective Woods. He appeared in the Police Court alongside another absentee, Henry Baker. He stated he 'did not recognise any military orders. The tribunal knew his views, and he repudiated any position he now found himself in. He refused to murder another man...'[23]. Citing his Methodism was unlikely to help his case. While some leading Methodists had spoken against the war, the church as a whole had declared itself in favour.[24] He and Baker were both fined and handed to the military. A few days later, Bert, who had been refused all exemption at his Tribunal, was 'arrested on military warrant without being taken to the police court.'[25]

Bert and Ernest were taken to Worcester Barracks, where they refused to obey orders. They were court martialled on the 14th November, along with two other Bristol men (Frank Pope, a leather roller also from Bedminster, and Henry Baker from Easton, who had been in court with Ernest).

22 A Literary Objector, *Western Daily Press* 27th July 1916.
23 A Hard Case and a 'C.O.', *Western Daily Press*, 1st November 1916.
24 *Blood and Guts: A Community at War*, www.methodist.org.uk/our-faith/reflecting-on-faith/conscientious-objection/blood-and-guts-a-community-at-war/.
25 *What Every Bristol Man Should Know*, Joint Advisory Committee for Conscientious Objectors, 1917, (Bristol Reference Library).

Evidence was given that they were apprehended at Bristol, and that they refused to put on their uniform when ordered to do so. They all pleaded not guilty and to prove that he was a conscientious objector one of the men said that he was the first man to arrange a meeting at Bristol to protest against the passing of the Military Service Act. They were found guilty, and sentenced to 112 days with hard labour.[26]

During Bert and Ernest's long absence, Annie Chappell and Florence Rudman would have maintained their household together.[27] We can imagine that they gave each other much-needed support. We do not know if either of them had children; if they did, they would have been small (3 years or younger in 1916).

Bert and Ernest were in prison together at Wormwood Scrubs, Plymouth & Ipswich—reappearing at the same court martials—for most of the war. They were each sentenced to a further 2 years in summer 1918. By January 1919 they had received 4 and 5 sentences respectively.[28]

While at Ipswich, Ernest went on hunger strike. Lois Bibbings notes that in 1919 'increased protests from the objectors remaining in prison and demanding release brought a wave of hunger strikes'. Force feeding was subsequently halted due to 'the increased risk of deaths occurring'.[29] Ernest's case was raised in the House of Commons in late March 1919: '[Is the home secretary] aware that E. Rudman, who is serving his fifth sentence as a conscientious objector in Wormwood Scrubs Prison, and who was recently forcibly fed twenty-eight times in Ipswich Prison, is now in a very bad state of health, having had influenza, pneumonia and bronchitis; and whether he will authorise this man's release on health grounds?' The reply was that the medical officer at the prison would make this decision.[30]

Throughout their long confinement, COs like Bert and Ernest were supported by comrades on the outside. Mabel Tothill, Secretary of the Bristol Joint Advisory Committee for Conscientious Objectors, wrote in June 1918, in a circular to imprisoned COs, 'I have recently visited Mr Chappell and Mr Rudman at Ipswich... and have been much cheered by

---

26 Bristol Conscientious Objectors Court Martialled at Worcester, *Western Daily Press,* 16th November 1916.
27 The house was still in Bert's name after the war as shown in Kelly's Directory 1919.
28 Pearce Register entries for Albert Chappell and Ernest Rudman.
29 Bibbings, *Telling Tales about Men*, p. 34.
30 *Hansard, House of Commons,* 27th March 1919.

Annie Chappell, mask performance from Steps Against War history walk.

them.'[31] This gives a suggestion of Bert and Ernest drawing strength from their companionship in jail; and the sense of comradeship in adversity which existed between COs and with their supporters.

Annie Chappell

Annie Chappell was active in the No-Conscription Fellowship (NCF). As Secretary of the Bristol branch, she held together a wide network of support for those who wouldn't fight. She organised meetings, signed up members, wrote to and visited COs in prison.

Will Gould, a friend of the Chappells, wrote from prison to his mother:

> A visiting order will be sent to you, but you must decide who is to come and peep through the bars at the roaring lion. Most of my male friends are in a similar position to myself. Mrs Chappell, I shall always be glad to see, but I must not make too many demands on her time.[32]

31 Letter to Ernest Batten, June 1918, quoted in BRHG *Refusing to Kill*, p21. (Original letter in Suffolk Record Office).
32 Letter from Will Gould to his mother, 24th Nov 1917 quoted in BRHG *Refusing to Kill*, p. 28.

Annie was among the women who played key roles in the Bristol Joint Advisory Committee for Conscientious Objectors. She would have worked closely with Mabel Tothill, who headed up the Committee, as well as Annie Townley and Bertha Ayles—all members of the Independent Labour Party. They brought a wealth of experience from varied fields. Some had connected, or been brought closer, through the campaign to build an alliance between the labour movement and suffrage campaigners in Bristol, to support a Labour candidate in 1913. Bertha Ayles had worked towards this in her role with the Women's Labour League. Annie Townley, an organiser for the National Union of Women's Suffrage Societies, had moved from Blackburn with her husband, a cotton weaver, to develop links between suffragists and trade unions. The campaign led Mabel Tothill, a middle-class quaker, suffragist and community worker, to form closer ties with these working-class socialists.[33] Annie Chappell likely had organising experience via the SLP. She may also have worked as a weaver before the war, at the Great Western Cotton Mill in Barton Hill.[34] Women working at the Mill were involved in numerous wildcat strikes and stoppages over repeated pay cuts and exploitative treatment by management.[35] In 1913 the National Federation of Women Workers supported a large and successful strike by the women for an advance in pay.[36] As the suffrage campaign had done, resistance to the war brought together disparate groups, sometimes leading to friction, but also to new understandings and connections.[37]

Some suffragists had prior experience in helping those who needed to hide.[38] SLP activists, who had links with Irish republicans and wildcat strikers, either had such experience or would soon need to gain it. A less documented aspect of supporting COs was directing runaways to safe houses and escape routes; this probably coexisted with the "above ground" work of some of these activists.

33 Hannam, *Bristol Independent Labour Party* pp. 13–16.
34 The closest match for an Annie Warren in the 1911 census is listed as "weaver, cotton works", as is her mother.
35 Richardson M, *The Maltreated and the Malcontents: Working in the Great Western Cotton Factory 1838–1914*, (BRHG 2016) p110–113. Richardson notes of one such stoppage, 'The company was particularly outraged at the women's defiant attitude in remaining in the winders' room 'singing and laughing throughout the day'. Apparently unable to resolve matters in house, the factory often took the women to court, where they were fined for breach of employment, or "damages" in lost profits.
36 Richardson M, *Bristol and the Labour Unrest*, p. 52.
37 We do not know Annie's views on the suffrage movement. Some SLP members supported it as an autonomous and militant struggle, while others argued that without broader economic change, it would mainly benefit propertied women. Rowbotham, *Friends of Alice Wheeldon*, pp. 18–20.
38 Following temporary release from prison '...many Suffragettes took the opportunity of freedom to remain on the run from the authorities taking refuge in a number of safe houses. Once recovered, they emerged unnoticed to undertake more militant 'outrages'.' https://www.museumoflondon.org.uk/discover/six-things-you-didnt-know-about-suffragette-hunger-strikes.

After the eventual release of most COs, Annie and Bert attended the National Convention of the NCF in London in Nov 1919. They were among the Bristol delegation, also including Fred Berriman, which proposed a motion: 'That in the future the NCF be established on an international basis, and that the organisation oppose Conscription irrespective of the form of government in existence.'[39] This last particular was probably a reference to the introduction of conscription in Russia by the Bolshevik government.

The Chappells moved to South Wales following the war, where Annie was an organiser for the British Communist Party[40], which formed in 1920. Inspired by the success of the Bolsheviks in the Russian Revolution, the SLP had entered talks with other socialist groups about merging to form a communist party. This was a complex and fraught process, with many on the left unwilling to take direction from Moscow, in addition to the existing differences between groups. Ultimately the SLP did not join—but many SLP members, Annie among them, did, some taking leading roles in the new party.[41]

Bert took up conjuring; possibly he had difficulty finding work in his former trade. (By 1939 he had work as a 'printer and cardboard box maker' in Cardiff, where he and Annie then lived.) He seems to have made a success of his magical career, as he was still performing in the 1950s.[42]

Gilbert Silverthorn—exemption on religious grounds

Gilbert Silverthorn, a boot maker, lived and worked at 53 North Street. This was just across the road from Walter Told, another war resister who ran a cycle shop at 62 North Street.

Gilbert's objection to being conscripted was founded on his religious beliefs—he was a Christadelphian. They are a non-conformist Christian sect with similar beliefs to Unitarians. On 13th March 1916 he put his case for exemption from combatant service to the Bristol Military Service Tribunal. It was reported that 'a tenet of the faith of this body was that no-one should take the sword'.[43] Though Christadelphians refused to fight they were prepared to do work that might be seen as supporting the war effort—even manufacturing munitions. This led to special provisions

39 *Agenda of the National Convention*, No Conscription Fellowship, London, 29th & 30th November 1919.
40 Information from Will Gould's family.
41 Rowbotham, *Friends of Alice Wheeldon*, pp. 100–103.
42 Information from Will Gould's family.
43 *Western Daily Press* 14th March 1916.

1916 Gilbert Silverthorne 53 North St. Bristol Exempt from Combatant Service

Artwork displayed in the window of 53 North Street during Steps Against War history walk.

being made for men who were members of this denomination.[44] Gilbert was granted exemption but required to do non-combatant service.

Christadelphians, along with some other groups e.g. the Quakers, were generally recognised by the tribunals as having well established religious beliefs that did qualify them for exemption on conscience grounds. At the time of the First World War there was a small community of Christadelphians in Bristol. Other Bedminster war resisters—Alfred Harris (Quaker), Albert Manns (Baptist), George Sampson (Plymouth Brethren), and Abraham Coburg (Jewish)—also claimed exemption on religious grounds.

Non-combatant service in Gilbert's case involved him finding 'Work of National Importance'. This took him away from Bristol and boot making. His first job was working in a nursery garden near Weston-Super-Mare, but he strained his back and was off work for some weeks. He was

44 Bibbings, *Telling Tales About Men*, p 38.

next posted to work in the Crumlin Valley Colliery in South Wales. When he left this job he was sent to do forestry work in Carmarthenshire. In November 1918, as the war ended, he became ill with influenza and then pneumonia and was allowed to return to Bristol.[45] There is no listing for Gilbert's shoe shop in the 1919 edition of Wright's Directory of Bristol and it can be assumed he lost his business.

Non-combatant service was not a soft option and frequently involved being assigned to do heavy manual work, almost as a form of punishment. There was the view that the work should be as harsh as what was being experienced by soldiers.

Fred Berriman — the absolutist's position

Fred grew up in Bedminster, the only son of William (Visitor to the blind) and Caroline (General Shop Keeper) (1901 Census). By the time of the 1911 Census we can see that he had married Ellen Jemina, had two small daughters, Carrie and Grace, and was living at 19 Hall Street near Parson Street railway station.

He was a compositor, one of the seven printers among our 40 Bedminster war resisters. He was a very active trade unionist and was the President of the Bristol Typographical Society from 1913–1916 and a member of the Trades Council. He was also prominent in the Bristol Independent Labour Party (ILP) and was its chair from 1912–1916 and from 1922 to 1925. Lastly, he was a member of the No-Conscription Fellowship.

As Chair of the ILP, Fred was one of the main spokespeople for the party at numerous public meetings around the city, giving full voice to its anti-war stance. The party's national paper the *Labour Leader* frequently reported on his activities. A report on 12th August 1915 shows that even in the depths of the war, an anti-war standpoint was gaining a large audience as well as some strong reactions:

> The biggest crowd of the season assembled at Eastville Park on Sunday, when a magnificent address was given by our chairman, Fred Berriman, on "Peace Terms". Towards the close an attempt was made by a soldier to smash up the meeting, but by tactful handling the meeting was continued and a good impression was made. There were good sales of literature.

45 Pearce Register.

Fred Berriman and comrade in prison, rod puppets from Steps Against War history walk.

Fred brought other talents to his political activities, as there are several references to him entertaining party members with musical acts. Even as the threat of conscription became imminent there was still space for some light relief as this report from Bristol branch of the ILP shows:

> We had a splendid programme of music on Sunday provided by Miss Winifred Smythe and Mr Fred Berriman. The hall was packed. We have thrown ourselves into the work of organising a no-rent-increase campaign, the first conference of which was a huge success on Saturday. We are also getting all organisations we can reach to pass No-Conscription resolutions.[46]

Fred was totally opposed to the war and was not prepared to fight, to co-operate in any way with the military or to do any work which directly aided the war effort: as such he was an 'absolutist'. In May 1916 conscription was extended to married men like Fred. In July 1916, he appealed on grounds of conscience to the Bristol Local Tribunal, and was granted exemption, being allowed to carry on his ordinary activities.

46 *Labour Leader* 18th November 1915.

But by November 1916 the Military appealed against this exemption and asked, 'that this man be granted Work of National Importance other than his present employment'. The Tribunal agreed to this, but Fred refused to comply and appealed to the House of Commons (Central) Tribunal. His appeal was refused, and he was given seven days to find 'Work of National Importance' or face being drafted into the Non-Combatant Corps. He neither found work nor reported to the NCC so in April 1917 he was arrested. He then refused to put on military uniform and was forcibly dressed by six soldiers. He also refused to obey any orders and was as a result court martialled and sentenced to 112 days imprisonment with hard labour which he served at Wormwood Scrubs.

He commented: 'Here one realised the brutality of the prison system, for we were subjected to bullying and every form of repression, and the slightest offence against prison discipline punished with solitary confinement and three days bread and water.'[47]

He was court martialled twice more and was sentenced first to a year and then two years hard labour at Dorchester Prison. He says of his fellow prisoners: 'There was a good proportion of Socialists among the sixty or so "absolutists" at Dorchester, and we spent the time allotted for exercise each day (which was the only time we were allowed to converse) in talking about our principles and ideals and comparing experiences in different parts of the country'.[48]

Fred was clearly given support by the Bristol Joint Advisory Committee for Conscientious Objectors, as he gets mentioned in the letters and reports of Mabel Tothill, its secretary. The Joint Advisory Committee also campaigned for the release of Bristol conscientious objectors, and Fred is listed in their 1917 leaflet *What Every Bristol Man Should Know*.

Fred was finally released from prison in April 1919 and resumed his role as Chair of the Bristol ILP. He went on to be a prominent figure in the Bristol Labour Party, served as a Labour Councillor from 1929 and became the chair of the Labour Group on Bristol City Council in 1937.

Fred was not the only 'absolutist' from Bedminster: there were several others including Bert Chappell, Ernest McDonald Paterson, Ernest Rudman, Ernest Roe, Ormond Pink, William Livingston and Walter Lewis. They all received physical and mental abuse both at the hands of the military and in prison. Most served sentences that stretched beyond the end of the war, well into 1919.

47 Berriman, Memories of a War Resister, p 2.
48 ibid.

Walter Henry Christopher Lewis—an international perspective

At the time of the First World War, the Haymarket (a small park) formed part of a large open space in the centre of Bristol. Just visible from the Haymarket in the south-west corner of this area was the complex of buildings on Bridewell Street that included the police station, fire station and the Police Court. It was the habit of Walter Lewis, who had been exempted from military service as a conscientious objector, to come to the Haymarket to make open air speeches to the passing throng.

On Sunday, 7th July 1918, these were Walter's reported words:

> Look what the Government has done. They have trampled on Ireland, suppressed three hundred million people in India, and I am here to speak the truth, although there is somebody here from the building opposite.... I don't care for Lloyd George [the Prime Minister], Arthur Balfour [the Foreign Secretary] or Hughes of Australia [its Prime Minister]. It is they who want the war to go on for many years. They are making a lot of money out of it. [49]

Walter was a tobacco operator and lived with his wife Mabel and daughter Edna at 15 Victoria Place in Bedminster. He described himself as an international socialist. His brother Fred (Victoria Lodge, Whitehouse Lane) was also a war resister.

When Walter made this speech, it was just over two years since the British Army and Navy had put down the Easter Rising in Dublin and most of the leaders of the uprising had been killed in the fighting or executed. But more pertinently, in the spring of 1918 the government had introduced a new Military Service Bill that could have brought conscription to Ireland and an Irish Home Rule Bill. The idea that home rule would come at the price of introducing conscription outraged republicans in Ireland. In response there were nationwide strikes and protests. Due to this resistance it proved impossible for the British Government to implement conscription in Ireland. In May 1918 the British Government responded by arresting around 100 leading members of Sinn Fein.[50] Support for Irish republicans was strong among British left-wing groups. Irish republicans were in turn active in smuggling war resisters out of the country.

49 *Western Daily Press* 16th July 1918.
50 Fitzgibbon C, *Out of the Lion's Paw*, (American Heritage, New York 1969).

Walter Lewis makes an inflammatory speech, tabletop puppet from Steps Against War history walk.

Walter's reference to India may have been prompted by events earlier in the war. In March 1915 the Defence of India Act, which had many similarities to the Defence of the Realm Act in the UK, was enacted by the Viceroy. It was used to suppress anti-war activities by the Indian Nationalist movement, particularly in the Punjab and Bengal. The powers enshrined in the Act were used to deal with the conspiracy to instigate a major mutiny in the Indian army in 1915. At Lahore, a special tribunal was convened and a total of 291 conspirators were put on trial. Of these, 42 were given the death sentence, 114 transported for life, and 93 given varying terms of imprisonment.[51] Support for Indian Nationalism was

51 Popplewell R J, *Intelligence and Imperial Defence: British Intelligence and the Defence of the Indian Empire 1904–1924,* (Routledge 1995).

apparent on the British Left at the time and there were a number of Indian women active in the suffrage movement here in the UK.

Walter attacked British politicians and the Prime Minister of Australia, William Morris Hughes. There had been a very active and successful campaign against the attempts by the Hughes government to introduce conscription in Australia.

Walter was correct in saying that 'there is somebody here from the building opposite' (Bridewell Police Station). Two police officers were in his audience making notes of what he was saying. He was arrested under the provisions of the Defence of the Realm Act, where it was laid down '...that any person who by word or mouth said anything likely to cause disaffection, mutiny or sedition among HM Forces or the civil population was guilty of an offence'. Walter was found guilty and a fine of £5 or 25-days imprisonment was imposed by the Police Court.[52]

This conviction then prompted the authorities to bring Walter before another Military Service Tribunal, where he was told to report to the Non-Combatant Corps. He appealed against this decision on 7th August 1918. He said that he, 'was opposed to force, believing in education to produce a sane system. He did not believe in force to enforce Government decrees. He was reminded of the force being used in Russia now, and replied that he is opposed to it even by a Socialist Russian Government.'[53]

Walter's comment on 'the Socialist Russian Government' should be seen in the context of the Bolsheviks coming to power in the October Revolution of 1917. From November 1917 Russia was thrown into a very bloody civil war. The counter revolutionary White Army opposing the Bolsheviks included British troops. Trotsky had imposed conscription in Russia in June 1918 to bolster the strength of the Bolshevik Red Army.[54] The Bolsheviks were also eliminating many socialists and anarchists who they saw as a threat to their absolute control of the Russian Government.[55]

Walter's appeal failed and again he was told to report to the Non-Combatant Corps. He refused to cooperate, was court martialled on 17th August 1918 and sentenced to 2 years hard labour in Wormwood Scrubs. We do not know when he was released.

52 *Western Daily Press* 16th July 1918.
53 *Western Daily Press* 8th August 1918.
54 Bullock D, *The Russian Civil War 1918–22*, (Osprey Publishing Oxford 2008).
55 Goldman E, *Living My Life*, (Dover Publications New York 1970) , 500 Anarchists Arrested, *Western Daily Press* 21st May 1918.

Going on the run

After 2nd March 1916 all eligible men were deemed to have enlisted in the military. If you were eligible and you failed to either obtain an exemption certificate from a Military Service Tribunal or report for duty, you were regarded as an 'absentee'. *The Police Gazette* was an official weekly publication which listed the names of all those who deserted or went absent without leave. It therefore provides some indication of the total number of absentees and deserters. As such, Cyril Pearce comments:

> ...the fact that between March 1916 and April 1917 almost 95,000 men tried to avoid military service is a salutary antidote to notions of a prevailing and unalloyed patriotic enthusiasm among young men to do their bit for King and Country.[56]

We don't know the numbers of Bedminster men who were 'absentees' or deserters, as many would have gone below the radar. We have here just a small sample who we know about.

Given that the chances of gaining exemption from combatant service by a Military Service Tribunal were very small,[57] and the likely consequences of then continuing to refuse to fight could be prison and hard labour, the decision to go on the run would appear to be a pragmatic choice. We share below the family memories of Sidney Vicary Vowles (204 North Street) who tried to escape to the USA.

For some going on the run was a political as well as a practical response to conscription. The anarchist paper *Freedom* commented on the first Military Service Tribunals in March 1916:

> Never before have we had such a spectacle of humbug and hypocrisy as that presented by the Tribunals ... To say that the whole affair is a farce is to put it mildly; it is more, it is a disgusting example of despotism in its most tyrannical and brutal form ... [J]udging the Tribunals by their first week's working, it is apparent that the best course for the man who has made up his mind not to serve is to simply ignore them.

56 Pearce C, *Communities of Resistance: Patterns of Dissent in Britain, 1914–1918* (Francis Boutle, 2020 Forthcoming).
57 *Western Daily Press* 21st Nov 1918 reported on the final meeting of the Bristol MST held on 20th Nov: It had heard 8000 appeals, 732 on medical grounds, a further 6693 were refused. 180 appeals went to the Central Tribunal of which 105 upheld the Bristol decision.

As we will sec, William Livingston (45 Vicarage Road) is a Bedminster man who did just that and who joined a group of London anarchists on the run in Scotland.

There were also those who, having enlisted, changed their minds about their preparedness to fight. This might be for religious or political reasons but in most cases it was simply because they could no longer face the horror and terrible conditions on the various battle fronts; often they were suffering from what we would now know as Post Traumatic Stress Disorder. Coming back to Bristol on leave would provide the opportunity to go AWOL (Absent Without Leave). Many soldiers were very young— we cite below the case of George Wilkins, a 19-year-old deserter (168 Bedminster Down Road).

There were also those who supported men on the run by sheltering and concealing them. In Bedminster, we have a prime example in George Edgar Barker, a cycle shop proprietor (12 Cannon Street) who was aided by Walter Told, another cycle shop proprietor (62 North Street). Their story is told below.

A CO escapes by ship, miniature theatre from Steps Against War history walk.

Sidney Vicary Vowles—a family memory of a man on the run

In the war years Sidney Vicary Vowles's home was at 204 North Street in Bedminster. He was a 35-year-old married man by the time conscription was introduced in 1916.

The following account was provided to Cyril Pearce by Margaret McGregor, a descendant of Sidney and his daughter Stella (1st July 2016):

> Stella's father was Sidney Vicary Vowles… Stella's mother was Lily Whittington, whose family greatly disapproved of her father so there was very little family talk in my childhood about him, his background and relatives. The primary reason for this disapproval lay in his political views. By profession a political agent, he had originally worked for the Conservative party but his convictions changed and he "changed sides" and became a Socialist. As Stella ruefully remarked many years later "no-one likes a turncoat". That his Socialist views were strongly and sincerely held there is no doubt. It was customary at that time for people with strong opinions to stand on the Downs near the top of Blackboy Hill "on a soapbox" and harangue the crowds. This Sidney did – Stella recalled sometimes being present. He was generous to a fault and would give away items from home which could scarcely be spared. His political views meant that he had no time for the church and its tenets. Stella was not allowed to attend Sunday School but instead went at one time to a Socialist equivalent. Her parents did not wish to have her baptised. This lack of religious faith displeased the Whittingtons ….

> Sidney's Socialist ideals meant that he was a firm believer in the "brotherhood of man" which meant that the concept of going to War was unthinkable. Later Stella was forbidden to join "the Brownies" because he regarded this as militaristic. Sidney was in effect a "conscientious objector" but when conscription came in for the Great War he did not register as such but decided to leave the country and head for America. His father's profession being Steam Packet Agent perhaps he had ready contacts. But it was not to be. The ship was torpedoed and "he had to swim for his life" since he returned to his cabin to get his money (presumably all he had in the world, intended to set himself up in his new life).

By the time he got back up on deck the lifeboat had left and he had to swim out to it. They were rescued but by a ship returning to England. Thereafter for the duration of the war he was "on the run" to avoid conscription…

Like most men who were absentees or deserters, Sidney was listed in *the Police Gazette* (16th January 1917).

Once the war was over, in the "Land fit for Heroes" even the heroes with impressive records of wartime bravery found it hard enough to get work, what hope for Sidney? He managed a succession of odd-jobs: a swimming bath attendant at one time and later, at the time of his death, some sort of caretaker with a tied cottage…[58]

Sidney died on 26th February 1932 at the relatively young age of 51 and was buried on 1st March 1932 at Greenbank Cemetery.[59]

George Wilkins and Alice Harver—the defiant deserter

George Henry Wilkins, nineteen, went missing from the army in late July 1917. Military Police called fortnightly on his mother, Alice Harver, at her house in Bedminster Down. Detective Woods also made regular visits, but they found no sign of George.

George was the youngest of Alice's six children. Their father, a miner, died when George was small. Alice remarried, to Charles Harver, a postman, in 1909. The 1911 census shows her also working as a postwoman. George, at 12, was running a greengrocer's shop with his 18-year-old brother Charles Wilkins, while Charles's wife Gertrude worked at the tobacco factory.

In November, almost four months after George's disappearance, Detective Woods caught up with him. The *Western Daily Press* of 21st November reports:

Detective Woods stated that, in company with PC Dempsey, he went to Bedminster Down Road, and saw the female defendant, and asked where Wilkins was. She replied that she had not seen

---

58 Account provided to Cyril Pearce by Margaret McGregor a descendant of Sidney and his daughter Stella (1st July 2016).
59 Information provided by his descendants.

CAPTURE OF A DEFIANT DESERTER ON A ROOF.

George Wilkins and Alice Harver, as pictured in the *Illustrated Police Gazette*, 29th November 1917.

him for about three months. Woods proceeded to search the house, and heard PC Dempsey shout. He rushed round to the front, but Harver slammed the door in his face and delayed him. Dempsey rushed after Wilkins, who climbed through a back bedroom out onto the roof. PC Dempsey followed, and eventually the mother came out onto the roof too. There was a struggle on the roof, and as defendant and the police were endangered, Dempsey got back into the room. The police tried to coax him, but he refused to come down.

According to the *Illustrated Police Gazette*, 'Armed with bricks, the man kept the police at bay for about two hours, and it was not until a fire escape was obtained that he was captured'.[60]

It seems Alice had a history of helping runaways. Detective Woods stated that: 'Some years ago they traced a naval deserter to the woman

60 *Illustrated Police Gazette*, 29th November 1917.

defendant's house and the man was eventually found lying between the wire mattress of the bed and the bed, on which a baby was sleeping'.[61]

The magistrates remarked that Alice '...had apparently done all she could to evade all law and order and had obstructed the police in the execution of their duty'.[62] She was imprisoned for three months. George was handed over to a military escort.

William Livingston—on the run in Scotland with the London anarchists

William Borthwick Livingston, a 21-year-old clerk, was one of four brothers living at 45 Vicarage Road, Southville.[63] All four were conscientious objectors. Alex, Douglas and John accepted Non-Combatant Service or Work of National Importance. William took a different path, going on the run soon after conscription was introduced.

William was a member of Bristol Socialist Sunday School: he is recorded (like the Chappells), as donating to the William Holliday appeal in 1915.[64] Hence he was connected to radical ideas and to widespread networks of practical solidarity. Another member, William Wall[65]—a clerk from Easton—became his fellow runaway.

The two Williams travelled to Scotland. They were camping in the hills near Kirkudbright with a group of other men, when they were discovered by police. On the 19th April 1916 the Dumfries and Galloway Standard reported that William had been arrested with five other young men:

> Something of a sensation was caused in Kirkudbright...when six young men, handcuffed in pairs, were marched from the station to the police office. They were respectably clothed, but presented a somewhat unwashed and dishevelled appearance. All sorts of rumours were soon afloat concerning them, the most widely current being that they were German spies.

> Police had been informed that 'a number of men had been seen prowling about...in the highest and wildest part of the hill country

61 *Western Daily Press*, 21st November 1917.
62 *Western Daily Press*, 21st November 1917.
63 Pearce Register, 1911 Census.
64 Wm. Holliday Defence Fund, *The Socialist* July 1915, via Pearce Register.
65 Wall is also listed as donor to the Defence Fund.

William Livingston and comrade pursued by police, crankie show from Steps Against War history walk.

between Carsphairn and New Cumnock'. A group of constables set out to investigate. 'After a tramp of eight miles into the hills they came on Wells and Evans, who were pulling up paling stobs [fence posts] to kindle a fire', and whom 'they arrested without much difficulty'. The constables 'saw the other men in the distance, and called to them to stop, but they took to their heels with the constables hot foot in pursuit. A wild and exhausting chase ensued and continued for more than four miles among the hills'. William and the others were eventually caught. As they were marched back to Carsphairn, they 'lustily sang *The Red Flag*', which, the paper notes, 'combined with the fact that each wore a piece of red ribbon in his coat, leads to the belief that they are Socialists, and that their intended sojourn in the hills was to escape the operation on the Military Service Act... As they were all equipped with sleeping bags, ground sheets etc, it was apparently their intention to make a prolonged stay'.

One of the men, Fred Dunn, was charged with failing to report for military service. He was fined £2 and handed to the military in Perth. William and the four others were found guilty of having lodged on a farm for six days without permission of the occupier. They were sentenced to 14 days imprisonment. As they were removed to prison, they again drew large and curious crowds. 'The prisoners seemed to be greatly amused at the interest they had excited.'

Two of the men arrested with William, Fred Dunn and Bert Wells, were part of a group of anarchist friends from London. The group were

$\mathcal{V}oice_{of}\mathcal{L}abour$

A PAPER FOR ALL WHO WORK AND THINK.

VOL. III.—No. 38.   APRIL 15, 1916.   MID-MONTHLY, ONE PENNY.

DEFYING THE ACT.

[Information · has reached us that a number of comrades from all parts of Great Britain have banded themselves together in the Highlands, the better to resist the working of the Military Service Act. In making a direct challenge to the Government they hope to appeal more forcibly to the British public to break the back of this Act. The following article is from one of those outlawed on the Scottish hills. In view of the likely gross misrepresentation by the patriotic press, we have no hesitation in publishing it.]

'Defying the Act' article in *Voice of Labour*, 15th April 1916.

connected to Freedom Press, an anarchist publishing house, and several had met while working for the Post Office. Fred Dunn was editor of the anarchist monthly paper *Voice of Labour*.[66] While on the run, he wrote an article for the paper with the title *Defying the Act*: 'A number of comrades from all parts of Britain have banded themselves together in the Highlands the better to resist the working of the Military Service Act...'

The article argues that conscription aims to 'crush the spirit of revolt so rapidly spreading' in the country, replacing it with 'the poison of militarism'. It advocates going on the run as direct action to make conscription unworkable.

> The Government has outlawed us, and out upon the Scottish hills we are living the life of the outlaw. This is the only logical course to pursue to fight such a Government... [W]e defy them to make us soldiers. Bold and resolute determination has broken and rendered inoperative Acts of Parliament before, and will do so again.

It frames their outlaw existence as an act of solidarity with, and incitement to, others facing conscription. So it is in its own terms a public stand, though not one accountable to the state or using its channels:

66 Heath N, *Dunn, Fred*, 2008, https://libcom.org/history/dunn-fred-1884-1925.

The object of our stand is not so much to evade arrest, as to give heart to those who stand alone. To await the closing in of the net around you in your own home is to court disaster and to defeat the object of resistance. Our resistance must be made public [to inspire] the desire to revolt against the conditions we are compelled to tolerate[67]

Lilian Woolf and Tom Keell, who were running the paper in London, printed the article as a leaflet with a run of 10,000. They were jailed under the Defence of the Realm Act for printing and distributing a leaflet which could prejudice recruiting.[68]

Not all of the six arrestees were necessarily anarchists: Rupert Cartwright (from London) and William Evans (from Wales) may have been SLP members.[69] There was a degree of affinity or overlap between these groups however, particularly in their opposition to the state, and their belief in direct action.

At the end of their two-week jail term, William and his friends were rearrested as absentees under the Military Service Act, the authorities having had time to look them up. Due to a lack of witnesses for the prosecution the case was adjourned for two weeks, and the men were released on bail of £5, which they paid. One of them, Bert Wells, was reported making an anti-war speech the following week. He argued that there was 'no real antipathy between German and British people, or even the soldiers...as had been proved by the fraternising that went on when there was a chance.' He said that after the war there would be strikes, and 'the military machine would be used to put those down, as it was used to shoot the Irish rebels.' He urged the crowd 'to resist military service in every possible form, and not to go into the army under any circumstances.'[70] Wells was the only one of the five to show up for their next day in court. He argued mistaken identity but was handed to the military and then imprisoned. The rest were declared missing, and warrants issued for their arrest.[71]

67 Defying the Act, *Voice of Labour* 15th April 1916; published in *Freedom* Centenary Edition Vol 47 No 9 (Freedom Press 1986); Cyril Pearce, forthcoming.
68 Sheila Rowbotham 2018, *Two Rebel Women*, www.brh.org.uk/site/articles/two-rebel-women/; Heath, *Dunn, Fred.*
69 Pearce Register.
70 Dockhead Oratory: Outlaw & Anarchist Denounces the Army, *Dumfries & Galloway Standard* 17 May 1916.
71 *The encampment on Galloway Hills: Five young men arrested leaving jail,* The Scotsman 1st May 1916; *Carsphairn Campers: Only Wells appears,* Dumfries & Galloway Standard 17 May 1916; Pearce Register entry for Bert Wells.

William Evans and Rupert Cartwright were caught again in June 1916, at Dundarach cottage in Pitlochry. Archibald McKinlay, a chauffeur who lived at the cottage, was arrested and fined for concealing them. They were found after 'voices were heard in the cottage, which was occupied by the accused alone. It was observed that the blinds in the cottage were pulled down, and the accused was also observed carrying in parcels, undoubtedly containing food, from Dundarach House to the cottage.' McKinlay said in court that the men 'got his sympathy because he objected to the Military Service Act on principle.'[72] Evans and Cartwright were handed over to the military in Perth.[73] They were imprisoned, and spent much of the war in work camps for conscientious objectors.[74]

Meanwhile, Fred Dunn had escaped from Perth army barracks and gone on the run again. He stayed for a short time at Whiteway anarchist colony near Stroud, with fellow anarchist, artist and former postal worker Emily Wilkinson. He then escaped to the US, where he taught at the Stelton Modern School in New York, and then ran a cooperative taxi service.[75] Emily's brother George Wilkinson had apparently also travelled to Scotland with Fred and Bert,[76] but must have avoided arrest, as there is no record of this. This suggests there may have been others, whose success in staying hidden goes unrecorded.

After his bail break, William Livingston disappears from the records for almost two years. It is not until April 1918 that he appears again in court, at Axbridge, charged with trespassing. This time he was handed over to the Military Authorities and was court martialled. He served 112 days in Horfield Prison with hard labour. After further court martials, he received a second sentence of 112 days, and a third of two years, which he was still serving in May 1919.[77] His fellow Bristolian, William Wall, was apparently never caught.

To stay free for such long periods, William Livingston and others like him must have had help. While camping and living rough was possible for a while, to live year-round they would have needed accommodation, as well as access to funds. As Sheila Rowbotham comments:

---

72 Englishmen flee to Scotland, *Dundee Courier* 3rd June 1916.
73 English Conscientious Objectors are sent to the army at Perth, *Dundee Courier*, 3rd July 1916.
74 Pearce Register.
75 Heath N, *Dunn, Fred*.
76 According to Lilian Wolfe (formerly Woolf), interviewed by Sheila Rowbotham, *Two Rebel Women*.
77 Pearce Register.

The anti-war rebels depended on a lived solidarity, relying on prewar political networks as well as on friends and family to assist the young men on the run... [78]

Cycle shops, a secret chamber, and secret agents

On 14th March 1917 George Barker, a cycle agent, appeared before the Bristol Police Court and was found guilty. The Court Record states that he:

> Unlawfully did commit an act prejudicial to the Defence of the Realm, to wit, during the 12 months last past, with intent to assist the enemy did construct, maintain and use an underground chamber at his premises 12 Cannon Street, Bedminster, for the purposes of hiding and harbouring persons liable for military service.

An extraordinary story lies behind this charge, pointing to the local police working closely with the military and acting on information coming from a secret agent. George Barker's action in creating the secret chamber is linked to another cycle shop proprietor, Walter Told, who lived and worked at 62 North Street, just 200 metres distant from George's shop.

George Edgar Barker

Born in 1878, George grew up in Bristol. In 1891 he was living with his family at 15 Ashton Place in Bedminster.[79] In 1903, he married Minnie May Brand.[80] At the time of the 1911 Census he was running a cycle shop at 78 South Street. By 1914 he had moved his workshop to 14 Cannon Street[81] and by 1915 he was operating out of 12 Cannon Street.[82]

In 1911 he stood in the Bedminster West ward for election to Bristol City Council for the Socialist Labour Party.[83] This affiliation to the SLP would connect him to the Chappells. According to Dr. Nicholas Hiley,

---

78 Rowbotham, *Friends of Alice Wheeldon,* p. 40.
79 1891 Census.
80 Marriage record for George Edgar Barker and Minnie May Brand
81 Kelly's Directory 1914.
82 Wright's Directory 1915.
83 *Horfield and Bishopston Record and Montpelier Free Press* 28th October 1911, and *Labour Leader* 24th November 1911. George only polled 182 votes as against the winning Liberal who polled 963 votes.

THE "FUNK-HOLE."

DUG-OUT FOR SHIRKERS IN A WELL.

A remarkable story of an underground chamber—a dug-out—stated to have been kept for hiding persons liable to military service was told at Bristol yesterday when George Edward Barker, the occupier of a small cycle shop at Bedminster, was fined £5 or in default ordered to undergo 26 days' imprisonment. The charge was that during the past 12 months he had constructed, maintained, and used an underground chamber for the purpose of hiding and harbouring persons liable to military service.

On the south side of Bristol where Barker's shop is situated the formation below the soil is red sandstone, in which it is comparatively easy to cut passages. Detectives stated that when they visited Barker's premises they found an old dry well covered with rubbish at the top. There was a means of descent provided by pieces of wood inserted in apertures in the masonry.

About nine feet down was a recently constructed passage leading to a six feet square chamber hewn out of sandstone. This chamber was connected with Barker's shop by an electric bell.

In September last when the police visited the shop concerning a conscientious objector the defendant refused information. Early in the war Barker harboured absentees who he stated would not be found when wanted by the military authorities. They were still missing.

Barker denied the allegation that he had harboured anyone.

Article in *The Times*, 19th March 1917.

George Barker, mask performance from Steps Against War history walk.

George had been described as 'a noted anarchist' by a secret service agent.[84] His anarchist sympathies are confirmed by his move to the Tolstoyan Anarchist colony at Whiteway near Stroud in Gloucestershire after the war.[85] George would not have been the only SLP activist who leaned towards anarchism.

When conscription was introduced in 1916, George obtained exemption from military service on business grounds as he was conducting 'Work of National Importance'.[86] However, the military and police regarded him with suspicion. In September 1916 a police constable called at 12 Cannon Street in search of a conscientious objector. George refused to give any information. He was alleged to have said 'the Government and army might go to ___[hell].' On another occasion Sergeant Reed of the Royal Engineers had contacted George when trying to find two conscientious objectors, named Platen and Gore. George replied that 'they were now in a place where the military could not get them'. [87] 'Platen' was probably Albert Plattin of 2 Hill Street, Totterdown who was a printer and a socialist/anarchist.[88] Plattin was a well known figure on the local

84 Hiley N, Personal Communication.
85 Breeden, *It wasn't all ...* pp. 36-40.
86 Pearce Register.
87 *Western Daily Press,* 15th March 1917.
88 Pearce Register; Mann and Malatesta, *Daily Herald* 23rd May 1912.

political scene: he chaired public meetings, ran entertainments for Clarion youth, and was active in the Bristol Workers' Freedom Group.[89] Following his disappearance Plattin was apparently not caught until summer 1918, when he was court martialled and imprisoned.[90]

They interviewed him and searched his premises. They discovered a secret chamber beneath the cycle shop by following the wires from a generator and electric bell. Detective Woods' testimony describes the entrance to the chamber as being 9 feet down a dry well in the back yard, concealed by a pile of rubbish. The chamber, which was about 6ft square, appeared to have been recently hewn out of the red sandstone. The detectives alleged that Barker said a man named "Told" may have assisted him in carving out the chamber. Tools were found in the chamber, but no-one was there.[91]

At his court hearing on 14th March 1917, George sought to defend himself by claiming:

> The chamber in the well was made in connection with explorations in relation to the Speleological Research Society...some 30 or 40 men assisted in the exploration, but not all at one time. [92]

The magistrates clearly did not believe this defence.

We know that George was a key member of the Bristol Speleological Research Society[93] (an early caving club). A letterhead for the BSRS in November 1914 gives 12 Cannon Street as the society's official address and George as its secretary. Another member was Moses Rennolds, who ran Lion Stores in Bedminster, and supplied the Society with much of its equipment.[94] In 1914, members of the BSRS, including George, had conducted a search of *Aveline's Hole*, an important archaeological site in Burrington Combe, Somerset. They discovered some very interesting bones from the Palaeolithic period. The custody of the bones then developed

89 Bedminster West Ward, *Western Daily Press* 14th October 1907; Cinderella Club, *Western Daily Press* 23rd November 1909; Wm. Holliday Defence Fund, *The Socialist*, July 1915.
90 Pearce Register.
91 *Western Daily Press,* 15th March 1917.
92 *Western Daily Press,* 15th March 1917.
93 Williams RGJ, Membership of the Bristol Speleological Research Society 1912–1919, *Proceedings of the Bristol University Speleological Society*, 1999, 21(3) p230–231.
94 *Ibid.,* p 226, '...as an ironmonger with a family connection with mining, he was certainly in a position to supply and assemble equipment required in the society's activities...' Moses Rennolds and his wife Topsy ran two branches of Lion Stores, one at 219 North Street and the other at 2 Warden Road. Thanks to Derek Knapman of Lion Stores.

into a major dispute between BSRS and Dr Fawcett of Bristol University. Correspondence from 1914 describes George as follows:

> This member, who unfortunately has possession of the remains, is a Socialist of the most pronounced type, and in our judgement, opposed Dr Fawcett purely on Class Prejudice.[95]

Moses Rennolds supported George in his stance. The dispute rumbled on through the war years until, early in 1919, it was finally resolved through a surprise visit to 12 Cannon Street by a group including the now Professor Fawcett. George was persuaded to give up the bones and it is recorded that: 'These he brought up from a well in his back garden where they were hidden'.[96]

Returning to George's arrest in 1917, what prompted the detectives to come to the bike shop on 1st March? The only clue in the press coverage of the case is George's unexplained statement to Detectives Woods and Wall that 'a man named "Told" might have helped him.'[97] Why did they ask George about Told, and why was Told not in court facing charges with George?

Walter Told

Walter Told appears in the 1911 Census as living and working at 62 North Street, Bedminster. He is described as a cycle maker, repairer and dealer, as is his boarder William Vaughan. He is also listed in the 1914 Kelly's Directory at this address. The Pearce Register shows that he appealed to the Military Service Tribunal in March 1916 for exemption from conscription on business grounds, but the Tribunal's decision is not known.

The *Reading Observer* (10th March 1917) in a report headed *'Escaping Military Service'* stated that a man calling himself James Ford was arrested and charged with giving false information on a form contrary to the Aliens Restriction Order[98]. The man came to Reading on 26th February and rented a bed. He had filled in the form giving the name James Ford, of 42 Kings Cross Road, and declaring himself as English. When challenged he finally admitted that the name and address he had given had been false and he was taken to the police station and charged.

95 *Ibid.*, p 230.
96 *Ibid.*, p 231.
97 *Western Daily Press*, 15th March 1917.
98 Required foreign nationals (aliens) to register with the police, and where necessary they could be interned or deported. This regulation was chiefly aimed at German nationals and later other enemy aliens.

This man was actually Walter Told. He explained that 'he was cycling from Bristol to London and stopped at Reading on the way. The only reason he gave the false information was that he objected to Army service'.[99] He was sentenced to two months' hard labour. We don't know if Walter's exemption from conscription had been revoked and that was the reason he was on the run. We also don't know if he was handed over to the military when he had served his two months imprisonment.

How does Walter Told's arrest relate to George Barker's arrest? The *Reading Observer* (10th March 1917) report states that:

> Enquiries at Bristol showed that he [Walter Told] was known to the police as an associate of men with advanced views detrimental to the carrying on of the war.

The researches of Dr Nicholas Hiley into the activities of the secret services in World War 1 have now linked these two arrests. Hiley reports that:

> At the end of February 1917 William Rickard of [the intelligence agency] PMS2 was in Reading, posing as a fugitive CO named "Cyril Wake", when he met a man calling himself "James Ford", who admitted to being another CO on the run, heading for London on his bicycle. "Ford" told Rickard about a refuge for COs built into the side of an old well, which Rickard thought sufficiently important to send a code telegram to his PMS2 handler, Herbert Booth, saying "COME AT ONCE".

Hiley goes on to say:

> Rickard's informant "James Ford" was arrested by the police, and PMS2 got them to ask if anyone should be informed of his arrest. When "Ford" gave the name of a friend living near Bristol, PMS2 realised that this was probably the location of the hideout.[100]

Walter was tricked into divulging the existence of the secret chamber to Rickard and then it would seem he went on to misguidedly give George Barker as the name of the person who should be informed of his arrest. Hiley states that Walter constructed the chamber with his friend George.

99 *The Reading Observer* 10th March 1917.
100 Hiley N. Personal communication.

PMS2, which came under the Ministry of Munitions, was just one of a number of competing organisations undertaking internal surveillance in the UK at this time and could be seen as one of the forerunners of MI5.[101] Rickard (also known as Alex Gordon) was an agent provocateur and informer employed by PMS2 who had been heavily involved in the framing of the Derby activist Alice Wheeldon and her family for plotting to murder the Prime Minister, Lloyd George. As 'Alex Gordon' he became notorious throughout the left and trade union movements across the UK, and questions were asked in parliament about his activities.[102] Herbert Booth was a key officer at PMS2, who was also active in the Wheeldon case. It was Booth who then went to Bristol to investigate and accompanied Detectives Woods and Wall at the arrest of George Barker. Unsurprisingly his presence was not reported in Court.

George got off fairly lightly as no one was discovered in the chamber. It should be noted that he was represented in court by a barrister—Mr Ernest Handel Cossham Wethered who was instructed by his solicitor Mr Reginald Nutt-Hamblin.[103] Wethered can be seen defending absentees and others being prosecuted under the Military Service Act.[104] This implies that George was given some support as it would seem unlikely that a mere cycle shop agent could afford to be represented by a barrister. From his comments in court it looks as if George was expecting a prison sentence: 'I suppose I shall have to go to prison for this. Make it as easy as you can for the sake of my wife, as she has to get her living here after I have gone.'[105] The court actually fined him just £5 (the price of a cheap bike or a week's wages for a skilled working man[106]) or in default he would serve 26 days' imprisonment.

101 Rowbotham, *Friends of Alice Wheeldon,* pp. 71–84.
102 *Labour Leader* 14th June 1917.
103 *Western Daily Press* 15th March 1917 and 1911 Census.
104 *Western Daily Press* 9th November 1916, 8th December 1916,12th January 1917. Wethered was also Chairman of the Bristol Munitions Court.
105 *Western Daily Press* 15th March 1917.
106 Hansard *HC Deb 01 August 1919 vol 118 cc2436-7W.*

Part 3: Consequences and conclusions

Costs and repercussions

The privations faced by the war resisters and their families were considerable and there were 'casualties'. By the time the war ended with the armistice in November 1918 there had been a marked shift in public opinion. The huge number of service men killed and maimed affected people in every part of the country. The state's control over people's lives and the seemingly insatiable demand for ever more armaments had resulted in a great war weariness. The actions of the war resisters were part of shaping the post-war consciousness.

Casualties

The men

It was the objective of the military authorities to break the men who refused to fight, which they sought to do by physical and mental intimidation, hard labour, solitary confinement and torture. In some of the Bedminster war resisters we have seen the impact of the escalating punitive response of the authorities to conscientious objectors. These men were broken in spirit, in health or both.

It was not a soft option to accept non-combatant service, either in the Non-Combatant Corps or Work of National Importance. The hard labour involved frequently resulted in serious health impacts. Gilbert Silverthorn (53 North Street) injured his back and ended the war with pneumonia. John Livingston, William's younger brother, (45 Vicarage Road) suffered a broken pelvis while working at the East Bristol Colliery. [1]

Many conscientious objectors were initially taken to a military camp, where if they refused to co-operate they might face physical and mental abuse. This might have been enough to break the resolve of some. We have one example in Alfred Thomas Harris (25 Chessel Street) of a man who, having sought exemption, may have been intimidated into accepting combatant service. The Military Records show he did go to the front and was killed on 12th October 1916 in one of the final attacks in the Somme offensive. [2]

1 Pearce Register.
2 *Soldiers died in the Great War 1914-1919* - Find My Past.

Sergeant proffers uniform to CO, rod puppet from Steps Against War history walk.

Once in the hands of the military, if individuals refused to obey orders and wear a military uniform, they would be court martialled and imprisoned. In the early days of conscription this would have been in military prison, but later COs were held in civilian prisons. The prison regime was harsh and included periods of solitary confinement. There were those, such as Sidney Pink (9 Dunkerry Road) who having initially taken an absolutist position then accepted being put into a Home Office work camp. We might speculate that he had succumbed to the brutal treatment and isolation imposed on absolutists in military and civil prisons and taken the option of the slightly less harsh work camp. Imprisoned COs who were judged to be 'genuine' could be transferred to a work camp, but most absolutist COs refused to make this compromise with the authorities.[3]

Imprisoned COs would serve their sentence with hard labour and then be taken back to military barracks, and if they continued to refuse to obey orders would be court martialled again and serve another period of imprisonment. This cycle continued till the end of the war with some of the Bedminster COs having served several sentences of 112 days or sometimes two years. Even when the war ended, release was not immediate. Indeed there was a view that COs should be at the back of the queue for demobilisation from the Non Combatant Corps and release from prison.[4]

3 BRHG *Refuse to Kill*, p 13.
4 No priority release for the "Conchy", *Western Daily Press*, 21st November 1918.

It was well into 1919 before they were released. Protests by the imprisoned COs (such as hunger strikes), and intense lobbying by supporters, were needed to gain the release of some. In the account of Ernest Rudman (25 Kensal Road) who went on hunger strike and was repeatedly force fed in prison we see perhaps the most extreme privations that were faced by any the Bedminster war resisters.

By the end of the war, in common with the soldiers at the front, the war resisters were often undernourished and in poor health, and in this weakened state were prey to the influenza pandemic of 1918–1919. Finding employment was a general problem for soldier and CO alike, but for COs the lack of a 'proper' war record was treated as if they had a criminal record.[5] Those who went on the run probably faced the greatest difficulties in finding work as we saw in the case of Sydney Vowles (204 North Street).

The women and children

We have no direct information about the fate of the mothers, wives and children left behind by imprisoned conscientious objectors and runaways. However, in this period many married women did not work outside the home, and they would in the main have been living in rented property. So to have no household income would immediately place them in difficulties, with the real possibility of losing their homes. They could turn for support to people like Annie Chappell and the other women on the Joint Advisory Committee for Conscientious Objectors. But even with this, the likelihood is that they would have had a very hard time and may also have faced hostility from neighbours. We can only imagine the need to seek comfort and solidarity from other women in the same position.

Mabel Tothill, writing in the ILP paper *Bristol Forward* in July 1916, made this comment following the extension of conscription to married men:

> Those who have wives and families, if they are not granted exemption, will need much faith and courage to persist in their refusal to accept any form of service inconsistent with their convictions. But unless we are prepared to say that a conscience is an expensive luxury that a poor man must forego, it is our duty to stand by them as comrades in the days to come.

5 Bibbings, *Telling Tales About Men*, p 129.

Horfield Prison in north Bristol.

Alice Harver (168 Bedminster Down Road), is the only example we have of a woman being imprisoned amongst the Bedminster war resisters. She was charged with concealing deserters, including her son George Wilkins, and obstructing the police. She was sentenced to 3 months in Horfield Prison. Several male war resisters also served time in Horfield. We can get some idea of what she faced from accounts gathered from suffragettes who were imprisoned during this period in Holloway in London. One woman's account describes how each day would start at 5.30 am. This was followed by cleaning out their cell, attending chapel and one hour in the exercise yard. Meals were eaten in their cells. An initial period of solitary confinement was the general rule.

During the first 4 weeks of imprisonment, the rest of the prisoner's time was spent in her cell, which was often airless, especially in summer; a certain amount of 'associated labour' had to be undertaken, which might involve making nightgowns or knitting men's socks. Once a week a bath was taken and twice a week books could be borrowed from the poorly stocked prison library. After 4 weeks, prisoners were allowed to take their needlework or knitting to the hall downstairs, which was more airy, and sit side by side, although talking was still forbidden.[6]

Aftermath

We have tried to get some idea of the degree of opposition or support amongst the general populace for the Bedminster war resisters. We have been unable to find any specific examples of antagonism towards them or their families from the public—which does not mean it did not exist.

On the other side we can see that support for the various political groups who took an anti-war position was sustained through the war and in the case of the ILP even grew in the final stages and immediately after the war. In the 1919 Bristol City Council elections[7], an Independent Labour Party candidate took the Bedminster West seat from the Liberals. The candidate, Edward Colston Millard, was a long-term ILP activist who worked for the Dockers' Union.[8] Though the turnout was low it is some indication that ordinary Bedminster people were far from antagonistic to war-resisters. In the same election, Bedminster East also went Labour and Walter Ayles, a very outspoken and well-known conscientious objector, was elected in Easton.

With the armistice in November 1918, most soldiers wanted to be demobbed and go back to their civilian lives. However, there was considerable nervousness in Government about the possibility of revolution and therefore reluctance to discharge the army too quickly. This caused great resentment among the soldiers. The strike actions and street protests of the Clydeside workers in Glasgow in January 1919 were perhaps the nearest the UK actually came to revolution. This resulted in the imprisonment of leading activists and the deployment of the army and six tanks onto the streets of Glasgow.

6 Purvis J, The prison experiences of the suffragettes in Edwardian Britain, *Women's History Review* 1995, 4:1, pp. 103–133.
7 *Western Daily Press* 3rd November 1919.
8 *Labour Leader* 18th July 1912.

This rising discontent also came to the streets of Bedminster at this time. The now very dilapidated and squalid White City on the edge of Bedminster was still being used as a barracks. The *Western Daily Press* (8th January 1919) reported that on the previous morning, 120 soldiers of the 12th Battalion of Bedfordshire Regiment marched through Bedminster to the Council House in the city centre to lay their complaints before the Lord Mayor. This could be regarded as an act of mutiny. They could not understand why they as infantry soldiers had been sent to Bristol to undertake transport work in the docks (doing civilian work for soldier's pay) or why their applications for demobilisation had been ignored. After gaining assurances that the Lord Mayor would take up their case they marched back to the White City. This protest was shortly followed on 11th January by 700 soldier mechanics marching from Filton into Bristol to again demand demobilisation. This was part of a wave of strikes and mutinies by soldiers across the country and amongst the forces still in France.[9]

By 1919 the civilian population was much more receptive to socialist ideas, and political groups and unions were keen to make their presence felt. The flavour of the time can be seen in this report of the celebration of May Day in 1919 in Bristol, published in the *Labour Leader* on 8th May:

> Bristol's demonstration was a huge success and one of the finest processions ever held in the town, accompanied by two bands and many banners. Several new banners belonging to the NUR [National Union of Railwaymen], ASE [Amalgamated Society of Engineers] and Dockers' Union made a fine show. The Socialist Sunday School banner, with a good muster of scholars, headed the Socialist groups with No-Conscription Fellowship and ILP banners.

The prominence of the No-Conscription Fellowship and ILP banners on this march shows quite clearly that the Bristol war resisters were not cowed by their experiences during the war. They were out there bearing witness to the stand they had taken.

These events show that by 1919 the patriotic fervour of 1914 had subsided. The dreadful realities of war and the desire to live in peace with social justice were now much more to the fore.

---

9 Rothstein A, *The Soldiers Strikes of 1919*, (Springer 1980) p. 51.

Connections

So, are we able to see that there was a network of resistance to the war in Bedminster? These 'connections' between the war resisters are summarised below.

Proximity

Looking at a map of Bedminster with the homes of all the war resisters marked, and even more so when you walk the streets and see how closely they lived and worked, it is evident that these people would have had numerous small day-to-day contacts with each other. In a time when in comparison with today, many more people walked or cycled to work, and did their shopping at numerous small shops on North Street and East Street, they would have encountered each other on a daily basis.

Take for example, Gilbert Silverthorn who had his boot-maker's shop at 53 North Street. He may well have had a few war resisters as customers. And he would likely have gone across the road to Walter Told at 62 North Street to get his bike repaired. So though their motivations for their war resistance were very different, one religious and the other very political, they were still connected by their proximity. The connection of proximity is even more obvious in immediate neighbours like Ernest McDonald

North Street, Bedminster.

Paterson at 54 and Thomas Hutchins at 52 St John Street, or George Sampson at 14 and Albert James Manns at 12 Nutgrove Avenue. George and Clara Sampson with their daughter Edna very likely encountered other war resisters, such as Annie and Bert Chappell, when they went to take the air in Victoria Park.

Places of work, and trades, would also have brought the war resisters and their families into contact with each other. There were at least 10 households with someone involved in the tobacco industry and 12 households involved in printing and packaging—most probably at Robinsons. So going to and from work, taking a break for a smoke, socialising after work were all times when people would have met up.

We are speculating here but when the geography of the area is closely examined and experienced it becomes hard to believe that these encounters didn't happen.

Political links

We have already shown that there was an active community of political and trade union activists in Bedminster in the pre-war period.

We know that at least ten of the Bedminster war resisters were politically motivated. We have shown that they belonged to trade unions, the Independent Labour Party, Socialist Labour Party, were anarchists, or were involved in the Socialist Sunday Schools. It is likely that more of the Bedminster war resisters were involved in left-wing politics than is shown by the documentary evidence. This political activism would in itself have linked the individuals, but we have also seen that there were a wide range of places where they would have come together. These political links are fundamental evidence of a network of resistance.

For many readers it may seem incomprehensible that so many men were prepared to go and fight for abstract concepts like 'King', 'Country' and 'Empire' and that their families let them go to the slaughter. What we have shown is that a network of people in Bedminster were willing to stand against the tide of popular pro-war opinion.

The hard information we have cited here is fragmentary. As artists we have taken the liberty of using our imaginations to fill in some of the gaps. But the evidence of the proximity of people's lives presents a strong likelihood that there was a network of resistance to the war in Bedminster. We have presented a complex web of possible relationships between families, neighbours, work colleagues, members of unions and political groups, and adherents to a range of religious beliefs.

The picture that has emerged runs counter to the popular image of a conscientious objector as the lone, educated middle class man of principle, stoically taking his stand against the war. What we have found is a community of very ordinary working people standing together and refusing to take their allotted part in the killing machine.

Appendix 1: History Walks

Here we provide the guides to two history walks so that you can navigate around some of the sites and homes of war resisters in Bedminster. You may also find it useful to refer to the map on page 51.

History Walk 1—Bedminster Bridge via Windmill Hill to East Street

This walk will take under an hour and a half and is just over 4 km in length. It takes in Victoria Park and Windmill Hill. It includes some steep gradients and there are a few steps on the route. There are seats in Victoria Park and on East Street.

You can view the route of the walk on the 'Bedminster War Resisters' digital map at https://www.brh.org.uk/site/article_type/map/. When you have opened the map, scroll down the menu on the left of the screen, click in the box beside 'History Walk 1' and then click on the subtitle for the route to be shown.

Start at **Bedminster Bridge.**

> This was a place where open air political meetings were held before and during WW1. It was also a meeting point for members of the Clarion Cycle Club.

Walk down the right side of Bedminster Parade passing the Rope Walk pub to the **Old Police Station.**

> Opened in 1882, Bedminster Police Station was, during the First World War, the home of B Division of the Bristol Constabulary. It is likely that some of the conscientious objectors and war resisters were temporarily held in the cells here after arrest.

Continue along Bedminster Parade going towards ASDA. Cross the road at the pedestrian crossing outside ASDA and turn right, then take the first left by the Barley Mow pub down Philip Street. Walk the length of Philip Street passing the Windmill Hill City Farm on your right. During the First World War there were a couple of **Tanneries** in the area to the left of Philip Street.

One of our war resisters, Frank Pope (74 Beauley Road) was a leather roller and might have worked here. The tanneries would have given the area a very distinctive smell.

At the end of Philip Street turn left on Whitehouse Lane. Cross Whitehouse Lane using the pedestrian crossing. **The Whitehouse** was here on this corner where there is now a small car park.

The Whitehouse was the home of Henry Herbert Frape, a printer's cutter and conscientious objector.

On the opposite corner was **Victoria Lodge.**

This was the home of Frederick Lewis, a grocer's assistant and conscientious objector. His brother Walter Henry Lewis (15 Victoria Place) was also a conscientious objector.

Go through the railway arch and turn right into Victoria Park, walking along the path that runs between an avenue of London plane trees with the play park on your right. The path climbs the hill, does a hairpin bend to the left and carries on to the top of the hill. Where the paths divide, take the central path towards a circular seat with a lamp post in the middle. In the WW1 period there was a **cannon from the Crimean War** on this site.

The land for Victoria Park was bought by the Council in the late 1880s. This was an obvious choice as the site had previously been used as a public open space and was also a favourite site for public meetings.

Now take the path up to the top between the bowling green and park keeper's lodge. At the children's playground turn left. (On sunny days you may be able to get a coffee here at the cafe van). When the paths divide bear right and go straight down the hill with the basketball court on your left. There used to be a **bandstand** here during WW1.

Political groups including the Independent Labour Party held open air meetings here.

Take the next turning on the right and leave the park through the entrance (with a few steps) onto Nutgrove Ave. Just a short distance down the hill are **12 &14 Nutgrove Avenue.**

Albert James Mann, a boot and shoe examiner and a conscientious objector lived at number 12. His neighbour George Sampson at number 14 was a dental mechanic and a member of the Plymouth Brethren. He obtained exemption from combatant service on religious grounds.

Go a short way up the hill and take the first left onto Elvaston Road, left again onto to Raymend Road. Just a short distance down the hill on the opposite side of the road is an alley that leads through to Kensal Road. When you emerge from the alley, turn left and you will see the houses on this side of the road are raised above street level. In this terrace is **25 Kensal Road.**

25 Kensal Road was a key household in the network of war resisters in Bedminster and Bristol as a whole. It was the home of Annie Chappell, Secretary of the Bristol Branch of the No Conscription Fellowship. Her husband Bert, a printer, was the Secretary of Bristol Branch of the Socialist Labour Party. They shared their home with Ernest and Florence Rudman, tobacco workers. In 1916 both Ernest and Bert were arrested, and court martialled together in Worcester as conscientious objectors and both served several consecutive sentences in prison. Ernest was force fed after going on hunger strike in protest for still being imprisoned in 1919 after the war had ended.

With your back to 25 Kensal Road, cross over the road and turn right and then first left onto Paultow Road. Walk down the road and at the T junction turn left. The first road on the right is Mascot Road and the house on this corner is **27 Paultow Road.**

This was the home of Detective Herbert Charles Woods who was based at Bedminster Police Station. Detective Woods was responsible for arresting a number of Bedminster war resisters, including George Barker (12 Cannon Street), Ernest Rudman (25 Kensal Road), and George Abraham Smith (68 Greville Road).

Retrace your steps back up to Kensal Road and turn left up the hill. On the corner of Kensal Road and Holmesdale Road there is a green area on your left. Take the path diagonally up the hill, through the car park at the bottom of a tower block. From the driveway here there is a **panoramic view to the south of Bristol.**

> During WW1, Bristol ended at St John's Lane running along the valley at the bottom of the hill. The hills to the south that are now the Knowle West housing estate were still farmland in 1916.

Go up the driveway to Somerset Terrace at the top of the hill. Turn left along Somerset Terrace going downhill. The road quickly becomes **Dunkerry Road and number 9** will be on your left.

> Ormond Sidney Pink, a machinist lived here. He was imprisoned as a conscientious objector and later spent time in a Home Office work camp.

Carry on to **32 Dunkerry Road** on your right.

> George Taylor, a sausage maker and conscientious objector lived here.

At the end of Dunkerry Road you come to a Y junction: turn right, going gently up hill. This is Cotswold Road: it bends to the right and just as you pass the highest point on your left is **86 Cotswold Road.**

> Samuel Charles Hall, a clerk/shorthand typist and conscientious objector lived here.

The road now descends steeply, on your left is an area of trees and greenery and, partway along a big stone wall, there is an entrance onto a footpath and a sign saying **St John's burial ground.**

> St John's was a main parish church in Bedminster and family members of several war resisters are likely to have been buried here.

Follow the path which goes down the steep hill through the burial ground. At the bottom you will come out onto a major road. Turn right, cross a minor side road and follow the main road, going under the railway. You will come to a major road junction with traffic lights. Using the pedestrian crossing—3 sets of lights—cross over to Malago Road. Turn right along Malago Road, pass a number of warehouses including Screwfix and just past Mr Clutch turn left up St John's Road. Go up the road and at the top there is a small terrace of houses on the left-hand side which include **52 & 54 St John's Road.**

> Thomas Hutchins, a letter-press printer and conscientious objector lived at number 52. His neighbour, Ernest McDonald Paterson, a tailor and draper, lived at number 54. Ernest was imprisoned as a conscientious objector.

At the end of St John's Road, you get a good view of the **Robinson Building.**

> At the time of the First World War, E.S. & A. Robinsons were major manufacturers of cardboard box packaging, and paper bags. It is likely that several of the Bedminster war resisters (particularly those involved in printing, such as Bert Chappell) or members of their family worked here.

Turn right into a dead-end road—you should be facing a small park. Follow the path to the left that skirts the railings around the edge of this park—this is the former churchyard of St John's. Take the first left down Church Road which leads down onto East Street. Turn left on East Street and cross the road to the HSBC bank. This is the site of **152 East Street.**

> Abram Coburg, a tailor from a Russian Jewish family, lived and worked here. He sought exemption from combatant service on hardship and probably religious grounds. Abram's brother Henry did join up and was killed in Flanders in 1917.

At the big junction at the end of East Street turn right onto Cannon Street where there is first a chemist, then a betting shop and the Robert Fitzharding pub. Somewhere beneath this block was **12 Cannon St.**

> In WW1, this was the cycle shop and home of George Edgar Barker and his wife Minnie May. On 14th March 1917, George appeared before the Bristol Police Court following his arrest by Detective Woods. The court record states that he: 'Unlawfully did commit an act prejudicial

to the Defence of the Realm, to wit, during the 12 months last past, with intent to assist the enemy did construct, maintain and use an underground chamber at his premises 12 Cannon Street, Bedminster, for the purposes of hiding and harbouring persons liable for military service.' George was assisted in the constructing the secret chamber by Walter Told, another cycle shop owner who lived and worked at 62 North Street.

Look across the road to the large Kustom furniture shop. This is the former **Bedminster Town Hall.**

Bedminster Town Hall was built in 1891. It was converted to a cinema by Ralph Pringle in 1909 becoming Bristol's second picture house.

Now retrace your steps back onto East Street and walk about 700 m down the street till you see a Superdrug and Poundland on the left. This is the site of **Bedminster Hippodrome.**

Bedminster Hippodrome opened in July 1911 as a 2000 seat music hall. George Barker (owner of the bike shop with the secret chamber at 12 Cannon Street) had a younger brother, Edward, who with his wife Daisy Barker were music hall artistes. They might well have performed at the Hippodrome. In 1915 it changed ownership and was converted into a cinema.

Continue down East Street and you will see a large red brick building and arched arcade on the left. This is the former **Wills Tobacco Factory.**

W. D. and H. O. Wills built their first tobacco factory on the site of a former tannery on East Street in the 1880s. Hundreds of Bedminster people worked at these factories. Four of our war resisters, including Ernest Rudman, and a further six war resister households had members of their families in the tobacco industry.

This is the end of the walk. If you continue down East Street you will reach the start point. You can catch buses to the centre and other parts of Bristol outside ASDA. There are toilets just inside the entrance of ASDA.

History Walk 2—Tobacco Factory to Cannon Street

This walk should take about 45 mins. It is about 2 km in length. The route is fairly flat with no steep gradients.

You can view the route of the walk on the 'Bedminster War Resisters' digital map at https://www.brh.org.uk/site/article_type/map/. When you have opened the map, scroll down the menu on the left of the screen, click in the box beside 'History Walk 2' and then click on the subtitle for the route to be shown.

Start at the **Tobacco Factory** at the junction between Raleigh Road and North Street.

> W D and H O Wills built their first tobacco factory on East Street in the 1880s. In the 1900s a second tobacco factory was built on Raleigh Road /North Street. Hundreds of Bedminster people worked at these factories. Four of our war resisters and a further six war resister households had members of their families in the tobacco industry.

Cross Raleigh Road and walk along North Street. Take the second turning on the left—**Gathorne Road.**

> John Shoreland Harris, a grocer's bookkeeper, lived at 47 Gathorne Road with his elderly mother. John was a conscientious objector and was successful in getting exemption from military service on hardship grounds as his mother was reliant on his care.

Carry on to the end of Gathorne Road and then turn right up Upton Road. Take the next turning on the left—just a few houses up on the left is **45 Vicarage Road.**

> This was the home of the four Livingston brothers: Alex, William, Charles and John. All were conscientious objectors. Alex, Charles and John, while refusing to fight, all accepted some form of non-combatant service. Unlike his brothers, William Borthwick Livingston, a clerk, went on the run with another Bristolian clerk—William Wall. In April 1916 he was arrested in the Carsphairn Hills in SW Scotland with a group of war resisters including some London anarchists. They were imprisoned for two weeks for having camped on land without

the owner's permission. William then eluded the military authorities and went on the run again till he was arrested in April 1918. This time he was imprisoned in Horfield Prison for three consecutive sentences under the Military Service Act, finally being released in May 1919.

Cross over Vicarage Road, return to the junction and turn left along Greville Road. Walk round the bend in the road and then cross over to **68 Greville Road.**

George Abraham Smith, a carpenter and trade unionist, lived here. He was arrested at his home by Detective Woods and appeared before Bristol Police Court as an absentee on 6th May 1916. In court he is reported to have said: 'I will not obey any military order. I would rather die. I am guilty before the law but not guilty according to justice.' He was imprisoned and later did non-combatant service.

Walk back along Greville Road and take the first left (a continuation of Greville Road). Walk to the junction with North Street and turn left. A few shops along is **204 North Street.**

This was the home of Sidney Vicary Vowles, a lecturer and election agent. According to his family, Sidney went on the run to avoid conscription. He took passage on a ship in an attempt to reach the USA. Unfortunately, the ship was torpedoed by a German U-Boat. He and many of the those on board survived as they were rescued by a British ship and brought back to the UK. Sidney then went on the run again and managed to evade the military till the end of the war.

Continue along North Street till you come to a Tesco supermarket, cross over to the other side and go up the left side of **Agate Street.**

Herbert John Pym, a fitter's mate and a conscientious objector, lived at 45 Agate Street. Herbert was from a family of domestic servants who had come to Bristol from Wellington in Somerset.

Take the next turning on the left—Parker Street—and go to the end of the road, turning left onto South Street. This will take you back down to North Street where you should turn right. Shortly you will come to **123 North Street.**

On the site of this modern dwelling was the home of a joiner and conscientious objector, Ernest William Roe. Ernest was from a family who were all in the building trade. He was a Member of the Amalgamated Society of Carpenters & Joiners as was another conscientious objector—George Abraham Smith, who lived at 68 Greville Road.

Continue till you reach **53 North Street.**

Gilbert Silverthorne was a boot maker who lived and worked at number 53. He was a Christadelphian and claimed exemption on religious grounds. He was given 'work of national importance' at a market garden, a sawmill and then a coal mine.

Look across the road to the left at **62 North Street.**

Walter Told, a bicycle shop owner, lived and worked at number 62. He assisted George Barker, another bicycle shop owner, in creating a secret chamber for those on the run from conscription. In 1917 Walter was arrested in Reading, as he tried to escape conscription by cycling to London. In Reading he had encountered a secret service agent who deceived him by pretending to be another conscientious objector. Walter divulged the existence of the secret chamber and this resulted in George Barker being arrested and the chamber being discovered.

Continue to the end of North Street, turn right at the mini roundabout onto Cannon Street and walk along till you come to the large Kustom furniture shop. This is the former **Bedminster Town Hall.**

Bedminster Town Hall was built in 1891. It was converted to a cinema by Ralph Pringle in 1909, becoming Bristol's second picture house.

With your back to the Kustom furniture shop look across the road to the Robert Fitzharding pub, a betting shop and a chemist. Somewhere beneath this block was **12 Cannon St.**

In WW1, this was the cycle shop and home of George Edgar Barker and his wife Minnie May. On 14th March 1917 George appeared before the Bristol Police Court following his arrest by Detective

Woods. The Court Record states that he: 'Unlawfully did commit an act prejudicial to the Defence of the Realm, to wit, during the 12 months last past, with intent to assist the enemy did construct, maintain and use an underground chamber at his premises 12 Cannon Street, Bedminster, for the purposes of hiding and harbouring persons liable for military service.' George was assisted in constructing the secret chamber by Walter Told, another cycle shop owner who lived and worked at 62 North Street.

Walk up to the London Inn and turn right into British Road. Walk up British Road and take the first right into Victoria Place. At the far end to your left is **15 Victoria Place.**

Walter Henry Christopher Lewis, a tobacco operator, lived here with his wife Mabel and young daughter. His brother Frederick (Victoria Lodge, Whitehouse Lane) was also a conscientious objector. Walter was an international socialist and was arrested in 1918 under the Defence of the Realm Act for attempting to cause sedition among the civil population, after making speeches in the Haymarket in the centre of Bristol. He was subsequently imprisoned as a conscientious objector.

This is the end of the walk. You can catch buses to the city centre and elsewhere by retracing your steps, crossing Cannon Street and going a short way down East Street.

Appendix 2: List of Bedminster war resisters and map

Surname	Forenames	Address	Map	Profession
Baker	William Reginald	34 Park Rd.	1	Clerk
Barker	George Edgar	12 Cannon St.	2	Cycle Agent, Cycle Mechanic
Berriman	Frederick	19 Hall St.	3	Printer
Chappell	Albert & Annie	25 Kensal Rd.	4	Printer's Cutter
Coburg	Abram	152 East St.	5	Tailor
Dangerfield	Richard Thomas	14 Ashton Gate Rd.	6	Order Clerk
Frape	Henry Herbert	White House	7	Printer's Cutter
Hall	Samuel Charles	86 Cotswold Rd.	8	Clerk Shorthand Typist
Harding	Ernest George	73 Essex St.	9	Bread maker
Harper	Frederick John	29 Hengaston St.	10	Litho Printer
Harris	Alfred George	252 St John's Lane	11	Tobacco packer
Harris	Alfred T	35 Chessel St.	12	Loader of export goods
Harris	John Shorland	47 Gathorne Rd.	13	Grocer's bookkeeper
Hillier	William T	12 Ruby St.	14	Grocer
Hutchins	Thomas	52 St John's Rd.	15	Letterpress Printer
Keddy	Norman B	27 Bartlett Rd.	16	Press Machinist
Lewis	Frederick	Victoria Lodge	17	Grocer's Assistant
Lewis	Walter HC	15 Victoria Place	18	Tobacco Operator
Livingston	Charles Douglas	45 Vicarage Rd.	19	Wooden Box Maker
Livingston	John P	45 Vicarage Rd.	19	General Packer

Surname	Forenames	Address	Map	Profession
Livingston	William Borthwick	45 Vicarage Rd.	19	Clerk
Livingston	Alex Graham	45 Vicarage Rd.	19	Box and packing case maker
Manns	Albert James	12 Nutgrove Ave	20	Boot and shoe examiner
Mason	Arthur	7 Cromwell St.	21	Builder's labourer
Morrison	David	158 Coronation Rd.	22	Clerk
Paterson	Ernest McDonald	54 St Johns Rd.	23	Tailor and draper
Pink	Ormond Sydney	9 Dunkerry Rd.	24	Machinist
Pope	Frank	74 Beauley Rd.	25	Leather roller
Pym	Herbert John	25 Agate St.	26	Fitter's mate
Roe	William Ernest	123 North St.	27	House and Ship's Joiner
Rudman	Ernest	25 Kensal Rd.	4	Tobacco Cutter
Sampson	George	14 Nutgrove Ave	28	Dental mechanic
Silverthorne	Gilbert	53 North St.	29	Proprietor Boot & Shoe Shop
Smith	George Abraham	68 Greville Rd.	30	Carpenter
Sprague	Sydney John	14 Elmdale Rd.	31	Tramcar driver
Taylor	George	32 Dunkerry Rd.	32	Sausage Maker
Told	Walter	62 North St.	33	Bicycle maker and dealer
Vowles	Sidney Vicary	204 North St.	34	Lecturer and Election Agent
Walden	Joseph C	19 Elvaston Rd.	35	Warehouseman
Wilkins	George	168 Bedminster Down Rd	36	Soldier
Williams	Henry Francis	Clifton Terrace	37	Lithographic Printer

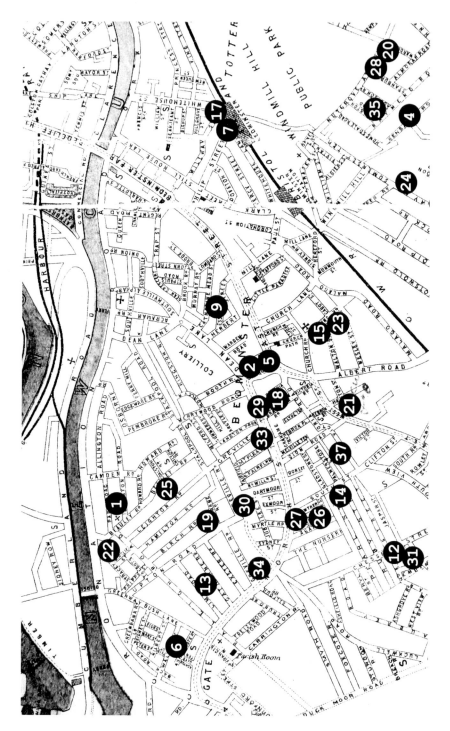

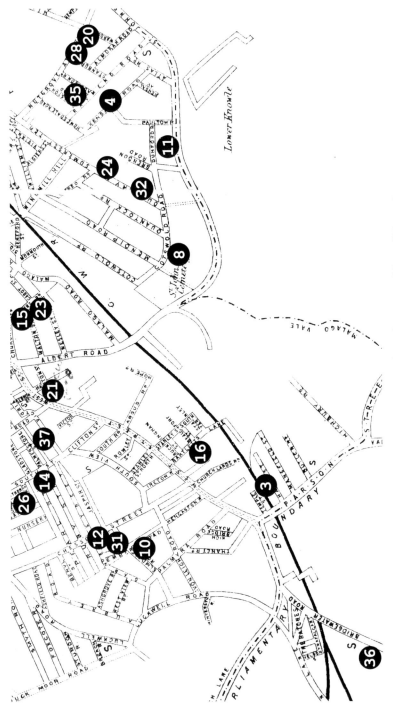

Bedminster War Resisters plotted on 1917 Map of Bristol.

Bibliography

Ball R. *Should Britain Go to War with Germany?* 2014, https://www.brh. org.uk/site/articles/britain-go-war-germany/

Bantock A, *Bedminster,* 2001, https://www.bafhs.org.uk/bafhs-parishes/ other-bafhs-parishes/52-bedminster

Berriman F. Memories of a War Resister, *Bristol Labour Weekly,* 30th July 1927.

Bibbings L S, *Telling Tales About Men,* Manchester University Press 2009.

Bristol Radical History Group, *Refusing to Kill—Bristol's World War 1 Conscientious Objectors,* BRHG Bristol 2019.

Brockway F, *Inside Left: Thirty Years of Platform, Press, Prison and Parliament,* New Leader 1942.

Bryher S, An Account of the Labour and Socialist Movement in Bristol, *Bristol Labour Weekly,* Bristol 1929

Bullock D, *The Russian Civil War 1918–22,* Osprey Publishing, Oxford 2008.

Burlton C, *Bristol's Lost City: Built to Inspire, Transformed for War,* Bristol Books 2014.

Challinor R, *John S. Clarke,* Pluto 1977, p. 22-3

Clarke A, *Taking the Pledge: the Temperance Movement in Bristol, 1830-1914,* Avon Local History and Archaeology, Bristol 2019.

Darwin B, *Robinsons of Bristol 1844-1944,* 1945, http://www.binson. co.uk/robinsons/robinsons.htm

Fitzgibbon C, *Out of the Lion's Paw,* American Heritage, New York 1969.

Forbes T & Byrne E, *Homes for Heroes 100—One Hundred Years of Council Housing in Bristol,* Bristol 2019.

Freedom / A Hundred Years—October 1886 to October 1986, *Freedom* Centenary Edition Vol 47 No 9, Freedom Press 1986.

Goldman E, *Living My Life,* Dover Publications, New York 1970.

Hannam J, *Bristol Independent Labour Party,* BRHG 2014.

Heath N, *Anarchists Against World War 1,* 2013, https://libcom.org/ history/anarchists-against-world-war-one-two-little-known-events-abertillery-stockport

Heath N, *Dunn, Fred,* 2008, https://libcom.org/history/dunn-fred-1884-1925

Horner A, *Incorrigible Rebel.* London, MacGibbon and Kee 1960.

Hunt S, *Anarchism in Bristol and the West Country,* Bristol Radical History Group 2010.

Hynes G, *Defence of the Realm Act (DORA)* https://encyclopedia.1914-1918-online.net/article/defence_of_the_realm_act_dora

McKay I, Ed. *Our Masters are Helpless: The Essays of George Barrett*, Freedom Press 2019.

Mullen J, *Wartime Popular Music,* https://www.bl.uk/world-war-one/articles/wartime-popular-music

Pearce C, *Pearce Register of British Conscientious Objectors in the First World War*

Pearce C, *Communities of Resistance: Patterns of Dissent in Britain, 1914-1918* (Francis Boutle, 2020 Forthcoming)

Popplewell R J, *Intelligence and Imperial Defence: British Intelligence and the Defence of the Indian Empire 1904–1924,* Routledge 1995.

Purvis J, The prison experiences of the suffragettes in Edwardian Britain, *Women's History Review* 1995 4:1, pp. 103-133.

Pye D, *Fellowship is Life—The National Clarion Cycling Club 1895-1995*, Clarion Publishing, Bolton 1995.

Quail J, *The Slow Burning Fuse: The Lost History of the British Anarchists,* Freedom Press 1978.

Reid F, Socialist Sunday Schools, *International Review of Social History* Vol. 11, No. 1 (1966), pp. 18-47.

Richardson M. *Trade Unionism and Industrial Conflict* http://humanities.uwe.ac.uk/bhr/Main/

Richardson M, *Bristol and the Labour Unrest of 1910-14,* BRHG 2013.

Richardson M, *The Maltreated and the Malcontents: Working in the Great Western Cotton Factory 1838-1914,* Bristol Radical History Group 2016.

Rothstein A, *The Soldiers Strikes of 1919,* Springer 1980.

Rowbotham S, *Friends of Alice Wheeldon*, Pluto Press London 2015.

Rowbotham S, *Rebel Crossings—New Women, Free Lovers, and Radicals in Britain and the United States*, Verso, London 2016.

Rowbotham S, *Two Rebel Women,* 2018, www.brh.org.uk/site/articles/two-rebel-women/

Weller K, *Don't be a soldier!* 1985, https://libcom.org/history/dont-be-soldier-radical-anti-war-movement-north-london-1914-1918-ken-weller

Williams RGJ, Membership of the Bristol Speleological Research Society 1912-1919, *Proceedings of the Bristol University Speleological Society*, 1999, 21(3).

Picture Credits

Pages vi, 5, 16 top, 24, 27, 30, 33, 35, 38, 41, 46, 52, 58: © Otherstory, 2020.

Page 6: Bristol Archives ref. 43207/9/13/12.

Page 9: Bristol Central Reference Library.

Page 14: comeheretome.com/2016/02/19/arthur-horner-the-welsh-conscientious-objector-of-the-citizen-army/.

Page 16 bottom: Bristol Central Reference Library.

Page 29: Bristol Central Reference Library ref. B32051.

Page: 47: Freedom: A Hundred Years 1886-1986, Freedom Press (1986), p19.

Page 60: historyofhorfieldcommon.weebly.com/horfield-prison.html.